THE HAMLYN
BASIC GUIDE TO

MACHINE SEWING

THE HAMLYN
BASIC GUIDE TO

MACHINE SEWING

Myra Davidson

HAMLYN

Dedication
To my students, for without them it would never have been born.

Author's Acknowledgements

My grateful thanks to Barbara Carpenter and Mary Straka for their much appreciated practical help with the text, Dawn Cloake for the diagram patterns in Part 4, and Margaret Wigginton for sewing samples.

I would also like to thank the following suppliers:
The Vilene Organisation for Ultrasoft Interfacing, Bondaweb, Wundaweb, Stitch'n'Tear and Fold-a-Band; Perivale-Gütermann Limited for Sew-all Thread; C M Offray & Son Limited for ribbons; Creative Beadcraft for crystal beads; Selectus Limited for Velcro; Rufflette Limited for curtain heading tape.

Illustration Acknowledgements

Front jacket: Machine embroidery by the author. Photograph: The Hamlyn Publishing Group – David Johnson. Sewing machine photograph courtesy of Frister and Rossman.
Back jacket: Embroidery and bedroom accessories by the author. Photograph: The Hamlyn Publishing Group – David Johnson; stylist Kit Johnson.
Frontispiece: Child's skirt and bolero. See page 61.
Colour illustrations: Sewing by the author. Photographs: The Hamlyn Publishing Group – David Johnson; stylist Kit Johnson.
Line drawings: The Hamlyn Publishing Group – Ray and Corinne Burrows.

Published in 1987 by The Hamlyn Publishing Group
69 London Road, Twickenham, Middlesex, England TW1 3SB.

Copyright © The Hamlyn Publishing Group, 1987

ISBN 0 600 50241 4

Printed in Hong Kong

Contents

Introduction

This book is a practical guide to Machine Sewing. It is a compilation of feedback from sewing-machine, dressmaking and craft courses that I have tutored at Adult Education Institutes and Colleges and of my experiences since my early training days some forty years ago. The aim is to give graduated learning, which will increase the reader's confidence as each part is completed. Every skill requires practice which is the only way to become proficient.

Machine Sewing is a self-educating/instruction book written in five parts, four of them representing practical sewing courses. The first part covers Basic Equipment, Knowing your Sewing Machine, Sewing Terms and Tips, and Pressing Techniques and Equipment, all of which give essential information. I have aimed at giving the instruction necessary for each stage of learning. Working through the book will enable you to master machine sewing, from sewing straight lines to making gifts with a professional finish.

If time is limited and it is not possible to work through all the graded Practice Plans, try to practice one or two processes each time you have a sewing session, keeping your samples for future reference, and first choosing the ones you will be using immediately. Read the relevant text through, and then again as you sew your sample. On the second reading, points that didn't appear straightforward at first will become clear, especially as you will be doing the practical sewing.

Follow either the metric or imperial measurements as a true conversion cannot always be made.

Abbreviations used in this book are:
RS – right side   CF – centre front   LH – left hand
WS – wrong side   CB – centre back   RH – left hand

| RS of fabric | WS of fabric | Interfacing | Lining |

I hope you enjoy working through the book. Happy Sewing!

MYRA DAVIDSON

Baby's toilet basket. See page 101.

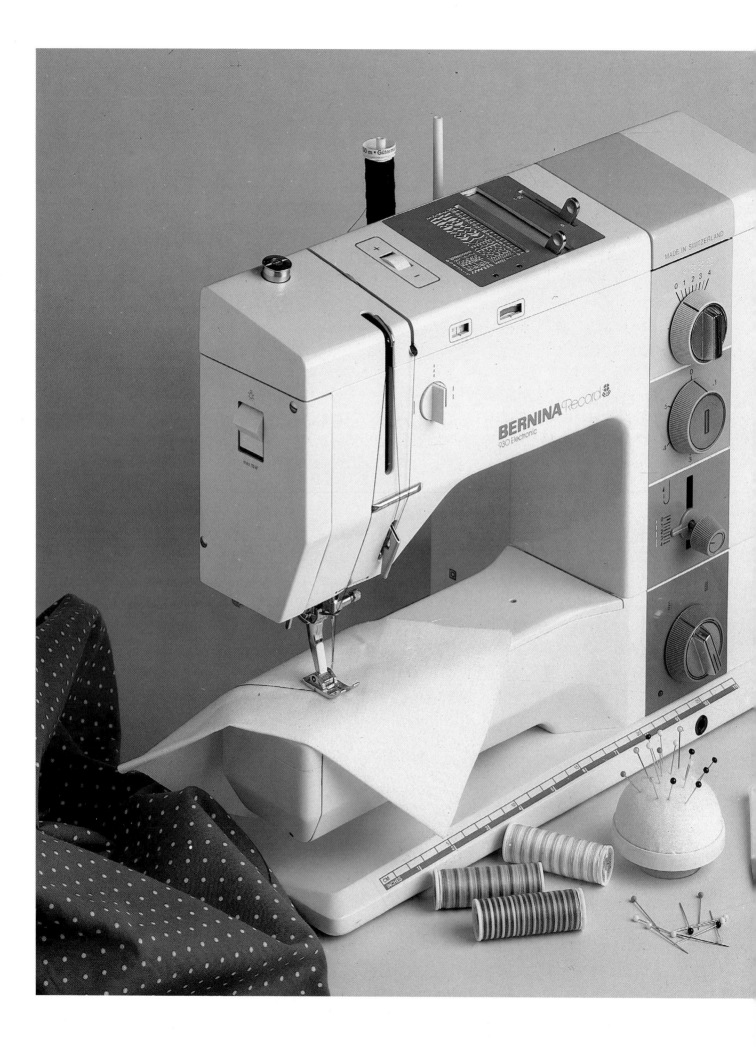

PART ONE

Essentials for Machine Sewing

Gather together basic equipment before you begin sewing.

Basic Equipment

When choosing the haberdashery items you need to start sewing, it is always a good idea to obtain the best you can afford. Not only will the items last longer, but they will enable you to achieve better results.

Scissors are the most costly item and several pairs are really required, because it is not wise to use any one pair for all purposes. Left-handed scissors are available, and it is advisable for left-handers to purchase at least a pair for cutting-out.

Cutting-out shears. Either 20 cm (8″) or 23 cm (9″) is an ideal size, and bent-handled to give a comfortable hold and a good cut. Made from forged steel, they can be sharpened and adjusted.

Medium-size scissors. 15 cm (6″) is a most useful size for trimming patterns. Ideally they should be reserved for cutting paper only.

Small scissors. For snipping and trimming seams, and cutting buttonholes. It is essential to have them sharp, right to the points.

Thread snips. For cutting thread only. Having these preserves the cutting edge of the small scissors.

Seam unpicker. The hook will pick up and cut a stitch to enable machine seams to be undone.

Tape measure. Made from fibreglass, which doesn't stretch. It's long lasting and has metric and imperial markings.

Sewing and knitting gauge. A small metal ruler 15 cm (6″) long, with an adjustable marker, that can be positioned to give precise, uniform measurements when turning up hems, etc. Available with metric and imperial markings.

Metre stick. Essential for marking long straight lines on fabric, ready for cutting out large items, such as curtains; useful too for a hemline to ensure that it is an equal distance all round from the floor.

T-square. For marking right angles on fabric and straightening the cut edge on material.

Tailor's chalk. A special chalk for use on fabric, available in tablet and pencil form. White and colours can be obtained.

Dressmaker's carbon paper. Special carbon paper that can be used on the WS of fabric. Three colours are in each pack, which gives a choice of a suitable one for the shade of the material being used.

Tracing wheel. Required for use with the carbon paper. Several are available, so choose one with a smooth wheel as this doesn't perforate patterns or snag fabrics.

Double tracing wheel. For marking the cutting line on fabric when using a pattern that doesn't give a seam allowance. It has two wheels – one which runs against the pattern, and a second with a small plastic bottle over it which is filled with powdered chalk. This wheel can be moved into any one of four positions, depending on what allowance is required. It leaves a trail of chalk to guide cutting out.

Pins. Fine dressmarkers' steel pins with highly polished points, 30 gauge × 60 mm long, are suitable for most fabrics and sewing requirements. There are specialized ones available: extra thin for lace; ball-pointed for jersey knits; and extra strong, thicker gauge ones for craft work – these are coloured-glass headed, making them easily visible.

Hand-sewing needles. An assorted pack contains a selection of length and thickness, which gives the beginner a chance to assess the length that is most comfortable to use. The choice of thickness is governed by the fabric – the thinner the fabric, the thinner the needle. Needles are numbered – the higher the number, the thinner the needle. Sharps are the most used all-round needle for general hand sewing, with a milliner's or straw needle used for tacking.

Thimble. Essential when sewing thicker materials, but it should be worn all the time for hand sewing, including tacking. Once you become accustomed to wearing one, you will find it impossible to do any sewing without one on the middle finger of your sewing hand.

Tacking Cotton. Absolutely necessary for all tacking, as it is a special soft thread which breaks easily and will not harm fabrics. The medium thickness (No. 50) is the most useful; it has a slightly hairy texture, which helps to make it stay in place until it's pulled out.

Sewing Thread. Choose it to match the material, or a shade darker, as it tends to appear lighter when worked into the fabric. The Sew-all Thread is synthetic and can be used on all materials. Mercerized cotton is available in different thicknesses and can be used on natural fabrics – the higher the number the thinner the thread: No. 50 for lightweight cloth; No. 40 for the heavier type. Other threads are available for specialized fabrics and processes.

Bodkin. A thick, blunt, round or flat needle with a large eye for threading elastic or tape into hems or casings.

Rouleau Turner. A very large bodkin sometimes with a ball end which can be pushed into a sewn bias strip. The eye is sewn to the fabric before going right into the strip to help turn it RS out.

Collar point turner. A wedge-shaped end to a short plastic ruler, used for turning collar points RS out without penetrating the fabric. It also has cut-outs to help sew buttons on with a shank.

Pattern paper. Marked in centimetre squares, used for making patterns from diagrams.

Cutting board. A very useful extra piece of equipment marked out in centimetre squares, which can be used for cutting out, and also when making diagram patterns and calculating fabric.

It is essential to familiarize yourself with your own sewing machine to discover its full range of functions.

Know your Sewing Machine

There are a vast number of sewing machines each with its own individual features, and yet all have much in common. It is essential to *familiarize yourself with your own machine* and to get to know the different knobs and levers that have to be set for various sewing techniques. *Use this book in conjunction with your own sewing-machine instruction book*, which will have a photograph or diagram of your machine listing the names of the various parts and instructions on how to fill the bobbin, thread the machine, set the length and width of the stitch, and so on.

Study each one in turn, fill the bobbin and place it in the bobbin case (or straight into the machine with some makes). It is necessary to follow these instructions in your book closely, as they will show whether the thread should wind off the bobbin clockwise, or anti-clockwise – only the correct way will give a good result. Thread and rethread the top thread so that the sequence becomes automatic. The stitch length (lever, dial or knob) will have numbers marked; some machines are marked 0–4, some 0–5, and older models are marked with stitches per inch. Stitch widths are sometimes set (narrow, medium or wide) with a lever – others with a dial system can be more finely tuned. Some machines need a

lever adjustment when switching from straight to zigzag sewing.

Your sewing machine will come supplied with some accessories, and more will be obtainable as they are required.

Presser Feet

There should be several presser feet – study your own manual to find out what you have and the reference names that are quoted.

All Purpose Presser Foot, sometimes named **General Presser Foot**, which some machines have, can be used for straight and zigzag sewing. Older models have a straight foot and a zigzag foot. These machines very often require the needle plate to be changed at the same time as the presser foot.

Most of the other presser feet are used for special processes:

Zipper Foot. Essential for sewing in zips, also used for making piping and machining it into place.
Blind Stitch Foot. For sewing a hem, using the blind stitch which is set by a lever or knob; it can also be used for edge stitching. Some machines have an attachment for the General Presser Foot, thus changing it to become the Blind Stitch Foot.
Buttonhole Foot. For working buttonholes, this has grooves cut out on the underneath to accommodate the 'beads' (see p. 17). There are several variations of the Buttonhole Foot, so it is necessary to follow the instructions in your own sewing machine book.
Embroidery Foot. A shorter foot with a clearer view of the work as it is being sewn. It has a cut away section underneath to accommodate close zigzag, such as satin stitch.
Quilting Foot and **Guide Bar.** A short foot, with a hole in the side to slide the guide bar in, with a screw at the back to hold it stable. Very often the embroidery foot doubles up for quilting.

The correct presser foot for the process being worked not only makes for easier sewing, but it gives a better result.

At the start of each Practice Plan, the machine setting states the presser foot to be used. For easy identification for all machines, 'General' has been given when straight stitching is going to be worked, and 'Zigzag' for zigzag sewing, although it might well be one and the same foot on newer machines.

Needles

Your sewing machine book will give you the 'system' number of machine needles to use, which has nothing to do with 'size' or 'type'. It identifies the one that is correct for the particular model of machine. The usage of the correct 'system' needle eliminates the possibility of an incorrect one causing wear and tear on other parts of the machine.

A good selection of needles is required as frequent changing is necessary to get the best results. Depending on the kind of fabric used, the quantity of machining worked, only two to three garments should be made with each needle. Several types are made. The ones required when first starting machine sewing are ordinary, ball point and superstitch/perfect stitch:

Ordinary/basic – Sizes 70–110 are used for a lot of everyday sewing.
Ball point – Sizes 70–100 have a rounded point, and are used for knitted and jersey fabrics.
Superstitch/Perfect Stitch – Sizes 70–90 are used on the more difficult-to-sew synthetic materials, woven or jersey. Using this needle will eliminate missed stitches.

Tension

All sewing machines are set for normal tension before leaving the manufacturers (or good sewing-machine mechanics after a service). They are tested having the same type of thread, top and bottom, stitched through double fabric. Your machine book will show diagrams of a perfect stitch, evenly locked midway between two layers of material, one showing the top tension too loose, and another too tight. Most machines have a top tension regulating dial, which can be adjusted, although it should only require a slight alteration. Make a note of the number it is set at before moving the dial. The bobbin-thread tension is adjusted by a little screw, either on the side of the bobbin case, or where the bobbin is placed in the machine. This rarely needs altering for ordinary sewing, and even if it does, a 'five-minute' turn should be sufficient – to the right will tighten, to the left will loosen the thread.

If your machine is not producing an even stitch, check all the following before making any alteration to the tension: top and bottom thread, rethreading both and ensuring the bobbin thread is winding off correctly; the needle is the appropriate 'system' for the machine, the right type and size for the material being sewn, that it is not blunt, bent or inserted incorrectly. If in any doubt discard the needle and change it for a new one, following the instructions on how to do this in your own manual. Test stitch through two layers of fabric to recheck. It is more often than not, either the needle or the threading up of the machine that causes uneven stitch tension.

Other points to remember

All machines require some cleaning. The fluff that inevitably collects under the needle plate and round the hook has to be brushed away.

Most machines need oiling and your instruction book will give a list or show in a diagram the points that require one drop of good quality sewing machine oil. Doing this regularly will ensure the efficient running of your machine. After oiling, run the machine on a piece of fabric before threading up, and make sure that there isn't any oil where it could come in contact with your fabric.

Sewing Terms and Tips

Terms

Appliqué – fabric applied to another piece of fabric, generally a shape to form a design.

Band – a strip of fabric to neaten edges, e.g. sleeve band or neck band. A ribbon band can be applied as decoration.

Bar tack – a wide close satin stitch worked at each end of a buttonhole.

Bead – a side of a buttonhole worked in narrow close satin stitch.

Basting/Tacking – temporary sewing of long stitches.

Bias – on the diagonal line, when fabric is folded 45° to the selvedge of the material.

Casing – a hem for elastic or a ribbon which is threaded through with the aid of a bodkin. A casing can be applied to a garment either RS or WS wherever needed.

Clean finish – neatening of raw edges on facing, etc., stitching over the raw edge using zigzag, or by turning under 4 mm ($\frac{3}{16}$″) and then machining.

Clip/Snip – short cuts into the seam allowance to enable a curve to lie flat. On an inward curve, clip well towards the stitching line. On outward curves, snip Vs out.

Dart – a fold of fabric which is stitched to give shaping. Depending where it is positioned, it will taper to a point at one or both ends.

Ease – to distribute, evenly, fullness from a longer length of fabric to a shorter length, without allowing it to gather or pucker. Always have the longer length on the top of the shorter one.

Ease allowance – the 'extra' that is required for body movement over actual body measurements. Patterns and designs will vary.

Edging – lace or trim with one straight edge and the other decorative.

Edge stitch – a line of top stitching worked very close to the edge.

Extension – additional fabric required as an over or underlap.

Facing – a shaped piece of self fabric to neaten raw edges. A separate shaped facing is required for neck and armholes. The facing for a straight edge, e.g. a blouse front, is often a 'mirrored' shape to the front and cut as one, which would be folded into place

during construction of the garment.

Grade seam allowance – trimming the seam allowance, each layer of fabric to a different width, thus eliminating bulk. Interfacing, if used, is trimmed close to the stitching.

Grain – the direction of fabric threads, lengthwise, running parallel to the selvedge, crosswise, across the width from selvedge to selvedge.

Hemline – a marked line at the bottom of a garment to guide where the fold of the hem will be.

Insertion – a piece of lace, ribbon or contrasting fabric sewn into garments or home items for decoration.

Interfacing – a layer of special fabric between the facing and the garment to provide shape and support.

Lapel – the upper front part of a garment that turns back.

Layering – another term used for grading seams to reduce bulk.

Layout – the way pattern pieces are placed onto material ready for cutting out.

Lining – a layer of material used to cover the WS of the outer fabric.

Machine basting – tacking with a long machine stitch, a feature of the newer machines.

Marking – transferring the dots, etc. from the pattern to the fabric.

Mitre – the diagonal join of material to form a corner.

Non-woven – material produced by methods other than weaving, e.g. knitted fabrics, Vilene interfacing.

Overlap – where one piece of a garment lays on top of another piece, e.g. waistband extension.

Picot – pointed decorative edging on lace or ribbons.

Piping – generally bias-cut fabric, folded in two, either with or without a cord inserted, often used to trim an edge or emphasize a seam. A woven piping is available and is used in a similar way.

Rouleau – strips of fabric sewn to form a tube and turned RS out.

Ruching – a slight gathering.

Ruffle – strips of fabric joined together,

then gathered or pleated and applied as a form of trimming to an edge.

Seam allowance – the margin of fabric between the sewing line and the raw cut edge.

Shank – length of thread between a button and the fabric when sewing buttons to garments.

Slash – a straight cut, which requires an applied facing to neaten.

Stay-stitch – a row of machine stitching, using normal sewing stitch length, worked within the seam allowance.

Stitch in the ditch – top stitching along the line formed by a seam.

Tacking. *See* Basting/Tacking.

Top stitching – machine stitching worked on the RS generally 6 mm ($\frac{1}{4}$″) away from the seam or edge.

Tips

1 Always test stitch through two layers of fabric to check correct selection of needle, thread and stitch length, when starting new projects.

2 Where possible have the bulk of the work to the left of the sewing machine, and position your machine to allow this fabric to rest on the table by the machine's side.

3 Do not watch the needle of your machine going up and down, but keep your eye on the edge of the material in relation to the marked lines on the needle plate.

4 If lines are not marked on the needle plate, place a piece of Sellotape by the side of the needle (taking care not to go over the feed dog). Remove the presser foot and using the hand wheel, lower the needle to the down position, and with a small metal ruler mark measured distances from the needle on the Sellotape using an indelible pen.

5 When top stitching, have the edge of the presser foot against the fold of the material or seam line, which will give a guide for maintaining an equal distance.

6 If you stray from the intended top stitch line, do not make a sudden move to correct it, but move gradually back so that it will not be too obvious.

7 When changing direction of stitching on a corner, leave the needle in the work, lift

Towelling bathroom curtains are easy to make and practical. See page 80.

The value of correct pressing cannot be over-estimated. As well as the iron and ironing board, pressing aids include (l. to r.) tailor's ham, sleeve roll and sleeve board.

the presser foot, pivot the work round, lower the presser foot and continue to machine.

8 It is very important to use the full seam allowance on all seams. If this is not carried out, garments or items will not turn out to be the correct size.

9 Work with the grain when pinning, tacking, machining and pressing – this helps to reduce fraying and prevent stretching of the seam. Always work on a garment going from 'wide to narrow' (e.g. hem to waist, armhole to wrist) – this will ensure you are working with the grain. Look at the pattern pieces as they are cut out to ascertain which way they should be handled.

10 Stay-stitching just within the seam allowance enables snips to be made, where two edges of differing shapes are to be placed together, thus reducing strain on one and puckering on the other.

11 When starting to machine, always hold the threads to the back for a couple of stitches. This avoids the risk of the threads getting in a tangle under the needle plate.

12 Cut tacking knots off and remove tailor's tacks before machining. This eliminates the possibility of catching them in the stitching and making them difficult to remove.

13 Remove tacking, where possible, before pressing.

14 When working with a thick material, use lining fabric for facings, pocket bags, etc. This helps to reduce bulk on the inside of a garment.

15 Place the pressing mitt on the end of a sleeve board to create a curved shape for pressing darts, etc.

16 A thick terry towel can be rolled up as a substitute for a sleeve roll.

17 Regard the iron as an aid in the preparation stages of sewing.

18 Whenever there are two of anything on a garment, always make sure you have time to do both at the same sewing session. They are more likely to be handled in the same way and so be identical.

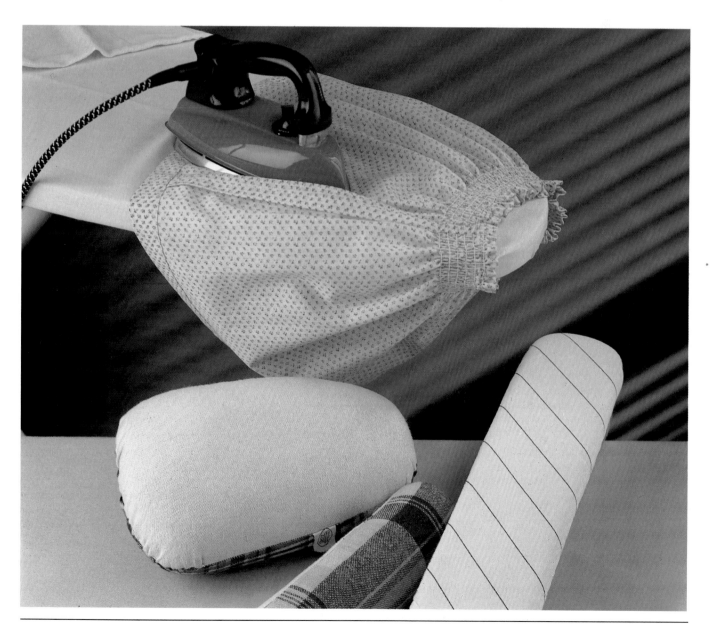

Pressing Techniques and Equipment

19 Only light finger-tip control of the fabric is required to keep it on the correct line for machine sewing. The 'feed dog' (the teeth set in the needle plate) will move it automatically without it being pushed along.

20 To thread the machine needle with ease, lick the thread, cut the end diagonally with sharp scissors, and thread the needle immediately.

21 When threading the machine needle on models that are threaded from the front to the back, prepare as above and hold the thread between both forefingers – one will steady the other as you approach the eye, then the thread will go through the eye of the needle without any problem.

22 Never thread a machine needle with the presser foot lowered.

23 If you prick your finger whilst sewing and get blood on your work, moisten a length of *cotton* thread with your own saliva, form it into a ball and roll over the blood spot.

24 Do not leave pins in a garment, or in anything cut out and ready to sew. The moisture in the atmosphere could cause the pins to go rusty and when they are taken out would leave marks, which would be difficult to remove.

25 Always throw away any rusty, bent, or blunt pins – they will only damage fabrics.

26 Use the hand wheel of your machine to position the needle correctly in the fabric before lowering the presser foot.

27 When sewing a difficult seam, round the neck or waist, etc., think of it in quarters – it will not seem so arduous.

28 Samples made working through the Practice Plans (pp. 23–37, 39–57) will be invaluable for reference. If a mistake is made during practice, you will realize what is wrong and, therefore, will be able to correct it when actually using the process.

29 Instructions in Part Five are in a more abbreviated form, with just a reminder here and there to pin, tack, machine, press, etc., but do remember good preparation is the foundation of good results.

30 When having a sewing session try to have the essential everyday chores done, so that they will not be on your mind 'to get to later'.

31 Do not continue sewing when you are feeling tired. Things are apt to go wrong if you do, especially when you are learning.

Pressing is the most important stage in sewing! The very best sewing will look nothing if it hasn't been pressed correctly. More time will probably be spent at the ironing board than at the sewing machine, and the result will mirror the effort. Pressing is a combination of heat, moisture and pressure, plus using the iron correctly with an up-and-down action; it must not be confused with ironing where the iron is pushed along.

The heat setting of the iron for pressing is governed by the fibre content of the fabric being pressed, but it must be hot enough to turn the moisture from the pressing cloth to steam.

Moisture is best provided by a piece of butter muslin, which requires soaking in water and wringing out tightly, so that it is 'damp' and not 'wet'. It can be used singly for most light/medium-weight fabrics; on thicker materials it will be necessary to be folded double.

Pressure is the amount of weight that the operator puts onto the iron. Only practice and experience will teach how much is required.

Pressing sets the shape of a garment; it gives sharp creases to any fold and flattens seams. Care must be taken to press sufficiently to give a good result without marring the fabric. Some 100% synthetic materials and those with a high percentage of man-made fibres, do not take kindly to a long session of pressing using a damp cloth, although pressing immediately with a dry cloth in place will help. It is sometimes advisable to allow the material to dry off naturally and then to have a further session of pressing.

Pressing aids

There are a number of pressing aids available which are generally acquired as necessary when doing more advanced sewing. The list below gives equipment in order of priority. Some items are, of course, already in the home:

Ironing board – preferably covered with a thick felt pad and cotton cover. (The coated covers that reflect heat are really not suitable for pressing.)

Sleeve board – a firm solid wood type is best for pressing with a similar cover to the one advised above. It is ideal for pressing small areas and especially baby clothes.

Pressing mitt – used with the thickly padded side uppermost worn on the palm of the hand.

Iron – medium weight. If it is a steam iron, use on dry setting for pressing.

Butter muslin – 1.50 m (1¾ yds) will provide three pressing cloths: two for using damp and one dry.

Sleeve roll – a hard roll which is an excellent aid for pressing sleeve and other seams.

Tailor's ham – a very hard pad shaped like a ham (hence the name!). This is placed on the ironing board and, depending on which way it is 'sat' down, represents the curves of the body.

There is further equipment available for tailoring and special fabrics, which is not needed at this stage.

Pressing tips

1 Several special pressing cloths are available and some do help to avoid shine on fabrics as claimed. But having spare pieces of fabric from the material that is being used, along with the damp and dry muslin cloths, is all that is really necessary.

2 *An extra covering on the ironing board* will very often help. If you are working with needlecord or corduroy always press on the wrong side and have a spare piece RS uppermost on the board; then when pressing, the two RSs will be together and the pile will not be crushed. A thick terry towel is useful placed on the ironing board when pressing machine embroidery or appliqué – this will prevent the work being flattened, as the stitches will sink into the towel. In fact, using this simple aid will make the stitching become more prominent.

3 *Always test press* half a large piece of spare fabric before pressing your sewing, to ensure that the *heat setting* is correct, that the right amount of moisture and pressure have been applied, and whether there is a tendency to 'shine' or not. If you are unsure about the fibre content of the material, do not set the iron temperature too high at first as it can always be increased. It is better to be cautious every time, rather than risk spoiling the fabric.

4 *Never* cross a seam with another seam before you have pressed the first, e.g. side seams on a skirt and bodice require pressing before the waist seam is sewn.

5 *Pressing a seam*. The correct procedure is as follows:

Keeping the layers of fabric together as they were for sewing, and placing the seam on the ironing board to enable the pressing to be carried out in the direction of the grain (wide to narrow) and, having a damp muslin in place, press the machine stitching in with a light pressure.

Placing the seam on the ironing board, so that it can be pressed open, and starting to open the seam with your fingers, place a damp muslin over, and with the tip of the iron only, tap your way up the length of the seam, keeping your fingers under the muslin, travelling ahead of the iron – this will start to open the seam.

Now press with the complete sole plate of the iron. If it is a *thin* material, place a damp muslin over and press. If it is a *thicker* fabric, put pieces of self fabric either side of the seam, butting them up to the edges (cut them to shape for curves), place a damp muslin over and press. By doing this, the level of the seam has been built up on both sides to take the width of the iron, thus avoiding indentation marks on the RS. A final light press on the RS, having first placed a piece of self fabric over the seam, will give a professional finish.

6 *Collars*. Pressing edges of collars and similar seams requires patience, as only a little can be pressed at a time. Place the collar RS down on the ironing board, and with a damp muslin in position, press just the edges using sufficient pressure to obtain a crisp edge, remembering to use the side of the iron only.

7 *Darts*. When pressing darts always have a damp muslin in place, press the stitching in on a flat surface, then place it on a curved pad, and press towards the dart point. To avoid an indentation mark on the RS, have a piece of self fabric folded and placed against the fold of the dart. Give a final light press to the seam line of the dart on the RS, having a piece of self fabric in place.

8 *Hems* are pressed on the fold edge in the preparation stage, and require further pressing when completed. A piece of self fabric placed raw edge to raw edge if it is a single-turn hem (or a folded piece for a double-turn hem) is required before the damp muslin is positioned for pressing, thus avoiding a line mark on the RS.

9 *Wool, wool blends, dark shades* in any material, or fabric that seems to have a tendency to 'shine' – when pressing have a dry cloth in place with a damp muslin on top before pressing, lift the iron whilst the steam is still rising and never allow the muslin to become completely dry. If you do overpress, hover with the iron, having a damp muslin in position, allowing the steam to penetrate the fabric. A further aid is to tap the steam into the material with the bristles of a clothes brush.

10 *Dry pressing*. A very few fabrics require dry pressing only. Always have a dry muslin cloth in place to prevent any damage to the material.

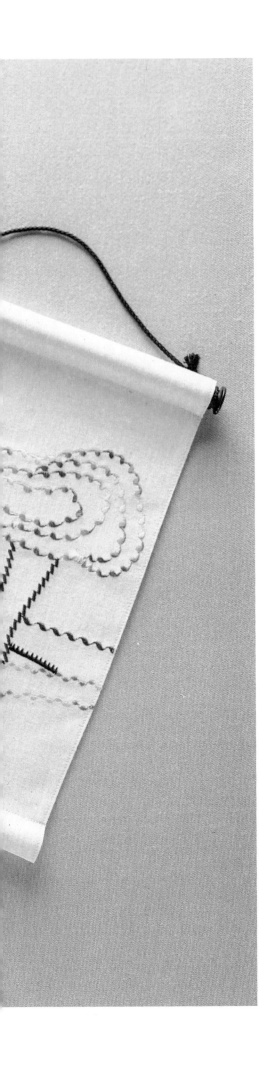

PART TWO

Practice Plans for Basic Processes 1–6

Rainbow wall hanging, bright and cheerful for a child's room. See page 103.

1a Straight Stitching

Straight stitching is used somewhere in everything you make using your machine, and to become familiar with how you can achieve good results gives confidence when you begin to make garments, etc.

1 Follow the diagrams and draw on to plain paper.

2 Leaving your machine unthreaded and having an ordinary needle (size 90 inserted), try out your control of your sewing machine using thin paper. Remember to put your presser foot down so that the paper moves forward automatically. It is more difficult 'sewing' paper than fabric, but you *will* be able to assess how straight a line you are keeping! Curves and corners can be practiced this way; your needle should remain in the paper at a point or corner, lift your presser foot and pivot the paper round, then lower presser foot and continue sewing.

3 Now progress to fabric, a firm, medium-weight, woven cotton such as calico is ideal.

Machine setting

Presser foot: General
Needle: 80–90
Stitch width: 0
Stitch length: 1–4
Set knob or lever for straight stitching

Requirements

Fabric: 32cm (12½") square
Thread

Instructions

1 Fold the fabric double so that you are working through two layers. Always hold the threads to the back of your work for the first couple of stitches to avoid any risk of the threads getting tangled under the needle plate. Work a row of machining with the stitch length 1, having the edge of the presser foot running along the fold of the fabric; do not watch the needle going up and down, but keep your eye on the edge of the presser foot and the fold of the material.

2 Turn to stitch length 2, position the presser foot against the first line of stitching, and work another row of machining.

3 Work further rows at stitch lengths 3 and 4, having the presser foot against the preceding row each time.

4 Turn the stitch length back to 2 and practice machining forward, but with a few stitches worked in reverse about every 8 cm (3¼"). Your instruction book will tell you which lever or knob to use to make the stitching go into reverse.

5 Work at least one more row to become familiar with reverse stitching. Practice further rows of straight stitching of your own choice.

1b Zigzag Stitching

Zigzag stitches have two uses: they are an excellent way of neatening seams which gives a professional touch quite easily, and decorative stitching can be accomplished automatically by using the controls of the machine to their full potential. Bed-linen and table-linen become more individual just by working a few rows of machine embroidery, and even one row worked on a collar can make a garment 'special'.

When working satin stitch or embroidery stitches, puckering can be avoided by using thin paper under your work, and tearing it away afterwards. There is a special backing called Stitch'n'Tear that can be used in the same way, and it works well with all fabrics. Backing is not necessary for practice on double fabric.

Instructions

1 Fold the fabric in two so that you are working through double thickness. Follow the diagram (starting with stitch width 1, stitch length 1), work 8 cm (3¼"), increase stitch length to 2, and work a further 8 cm (3¼"). Continue in this manner, altering the stitch length to 3 and then 4, to finish the first row of zigzag. You will note that as you increase the length of the stitch the zigzag becomes more spaced.

2 Select stitch width 2 for the second row and work through the stitch lengths as before, going on to a further two rows with

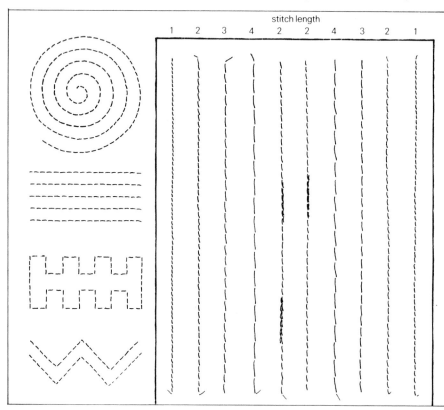

(Left) **Paper Exercises** *Enlarge shapes when drawing on to paper.*

(Right) **Straight Stitching**

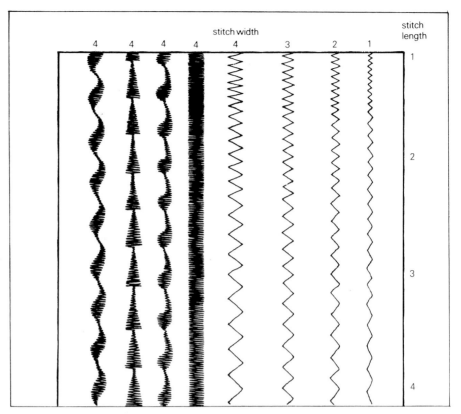

Machine setting

Presser foot: Zigzag
Needle: 80–90
Stitch width: 1–4
Stitch length: 1–4
Set knob or lever for zigzag stitch. (If your machine has more than one needle plate, make sure you have the appropriate one in position.)

Requirements

Fabric: 32cm (12½″) square, plus smaller piece for testing satin stitch setting.
Thread

stitch width 3 and then 4. If your machine has narrow, medium and wide width settings for zigzag, instead of a numbered dial, work through these following the instructions for setting the stitch lengths.
3 Leaving the stitch width set at 4 (or wide), select the stitch length near to 0 to give a close zigzag for satin stitch. Refer to your machine manual for instructions on altering the tension. (**Note:** With some machines you have to loosen the top tension, some require the bobbin tension to be increased by a screw on the bobbin case, whilst some need the hole in the finger of the bobbin case to be threaded with the lower thread. Whatever adjustment you have to make, it is best done gradually, always making a note of the original position of dial, lever or screw. Take extra care when altering the latter and only adjust 'five minutes' at a time.) Check your setting on the small piece of fabric, folded double, correcting the closeness of the stitch, etc., if necessary.
4 Now work a row of satin stitch on your sample – also try out any automatic stitches you have on your machine. Remember it takes time and practice to have success with machine embroidery, but the effect that you can achieve makes it worthwhile.

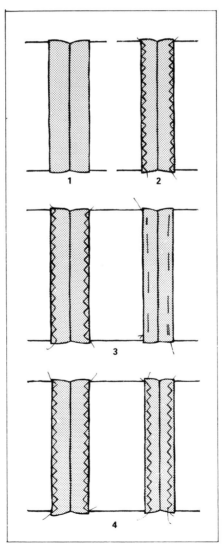

Open Seam 1 *Pressed open.* **2** *Raw edges neatened.* **3** *Second seam, raw edges turned under and tacked.* **4** *Second seam neatened.*

2a Open Seams

The plain, open seam is the most frequently used when making garments. To sew a good seam, pin, tack, machine, press, neaten and press again. The fabric being used dictates the method of neatening. Thicker fabrics are neatened using the zigzag stitch on the raw edge, while thin fabrics are better with the raw edges turned under before neatening.

Machine setting

Presser foot: General/Zigzag
Needle: 80–90
Stitch width: 0 for straight stitch, and 2–3 for zigzag
Stitch length: 2–2½

Requirements

Fabric: 3 pieces – 30 cm (12″) × 15 cm (6″)
Tacking cotton
Thread

Instructions

1 Place two of the pieces of fabric RS together, using the 30 cm (12″) for the length of the seam and having the raw edges even.

2 Pin, tack and machine the seam 1.5 cm ($\frac{5}{8}''$) from the raw edges and press the seam open.

3 Set the machine for zigzag sewing, and place one of the raw edges of the seam under the presser foot; work the machine using the hand-wheel for a couple of stitches to ensure the needle goes down by the side of the fabric on the swing to the right, and into the fabric on the swing to the left.

4 Neaten the other raw edge of the seam in the same way.

5 Set machine for straight stitching and sew another seam using the third piece of fabric.

6 After pressing the seam open, turn the raw edges under 4 mm ($\frac{3}{16}''$), tack and press.

7 Set the machine for zigzag. Place a tacked edge under the presser foot to neaten making sure, by using the hand-wheel, that the needle will pierce the fabric both on the swing to the right and the left.

8 Work the other tacked edge in the same way, take out tacking and give a final press to both seams.

2b Run and Fell Seams

This is a strong seam which is very suitable for frequently washed garments made of light/medium-weight fabrics. It is most useful on shirts, pyjamas, children's dungarees, etc., and to some degree makes a decorative seam. If you wish this to be more pronounced, then use a thread in a contrasting colour to the fabric.

Machine setting

Presser foot: General
Needle: 80–90
Stitch width: 0
Stitch length: 2–2$\frac{1}{2}$

Requirements

Fabric: 2 pieces – 30 cm (12″) × 15 cm (6″)
Tacking cotton
Thread

Run and Fell Seam **1** *Seam machined with WS together.* **2** *Half seam allowance on one side trimmed away.* **3** *Raw edge turned under and tacked.* **4** *Finished seam showing RS.*

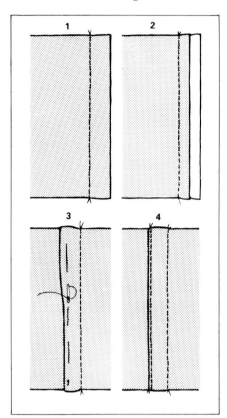

Instructions

1 Place the two pieces of fabric WS together, having the raw edges even.

2 Pin, tack and machine the seam 1.5 cm ($\frac{5}{8}''$) from the raw edge, using the guideline on the needle plate.

3 Trim away half the seam allowance on one side only.

4 Press the seam to one side, having the wider seam allowance on the top (on garments, this seam would be pressed towards the back).

5 Neaten the seam by turning under 6 mm ($\frac{1}{4}''$) and tack it down, making sure the folded edge is at an equal distance from the first row of stitching all along the seam.

6 Press the folded edge, machine, take out tacking and press again.

2c Mock Run and Fell Seams

As the name suggests the Mock Run and Fell Seam is similar to the previous seam, but less preparation is required, so it can be worked more speedily. It can be used for garments as suggested in **2b**, and also on

Mock Run and Fell Seam **1** *Seam allowance trimmed on one side only.* **2** *Seam pressed to one side, raw edge neatened, seam tacked down.* **3** *Seam ready for top stitching from RS.* **4** *Seam completed.*

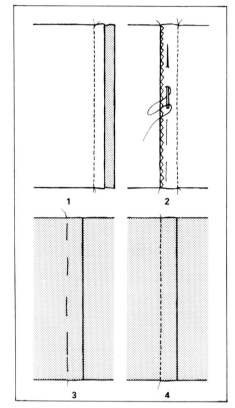

thicker fabrics where a felled seam is appropriate.

Instructions

1 Place the two pieces of fabric RS together, having the raw edges even.

2 Pin, tack and machine the seam 1.5 cm ($\frac{5}{8}''$) from the raw edges, using the guideline on the needle plate.

3 Trim away half the seam allowance on one side only, press seam to one side with the wider seam allowance on top (**Note:**

Machine setting

Presser foot: General/Zigzag
Needle: 80–90
Stitch width: 0 for straight stitch, and 2$\frac{1}{2}$ for zigzag
Stitch length: 2–2$\frac{1}{2}$

Requirements

Fabric: 2 pieces – 30 cm (12″) × 15 cm (6″)
Tacking cotton
Thread

This would be going towards the back on a garment).

4 Neaten the edge of the wider seam allowance, using a zigzag stitch over the raw edge.

5 Tack this down and, working from the RS, top stitch, keeping an equal distance from the actual seam. The presser foot can act as a guide, by placing it along the seam line.

6 Take out tacking and press.

2d French Seams

When using lightweight or sheer fabrics, this is a good seam to use for lingerie, infants' and children's clothes, as well as for straight seams in ladies' blouses and dresses. It is a seam which completely encloses the raw edges.

> ### Machine setting
> *Presser foot:* General
> *Needle:* 80–90
> *Stitch width:* 0
> *Stitch length:* 2 (approx.)
>
> ### Requirements
> *Fabric:* 2 pieces – 30 cm
> (12″) × 15 cm (6″)
> *Tacking cotton*
> *Thread*

Instructions

1 Place the two pieces WS together, pin, tack and machine 9 mm (⅜″) from raw edge, then trim seam allowance to 4 mm (³⁄₁₆″).

2 Turn the fabric so that the RS are together; make sure the seam line is on the edge by rolling the seam between fingers and thumbs (moisten them first in order to grip the fabric).

3 Tack as you work along the seam, press, then machine 6 mm (¼″) from the edge.

4 Finally, press the seam to one side, which would be towards the back on a garment.

French Seam **1** *Seam machined with WS together and trimmed.* **2** *Seam line rolled to edge and tacked.* **3** *Seam machined and pressed to one side.*

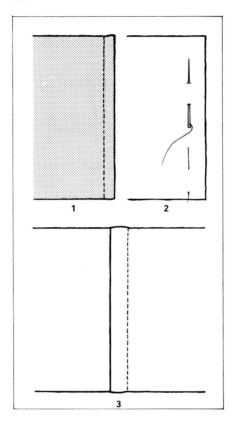

2e Narrow Seams

Suitable for seams on jersey fabrics, as well as on curves in any fabric, such as a crotch seam in trousers, or an underarm seam where the sleeves are cut in one with the bodice, as in a batwing sleeve.

Instructions

1 Place the two pieces of fabric RS together, having the raw edges even. Pin, tack and, with a small zigzag stitch, machine 1.5 cm (⅝″) from raw edges, then machine a second row of zigzag 1.3 cm (½″) from raw edges.

2 Trim off surplus fabric near this second line of stitching.

3 Set your machine for a wider zigzag and neaten the edges together.

4 Press to one side.

Some jersey fabrics have a tendency to stretch out of shape whilst machining.
To prevent this –

1 Take a length of sewing thread and lay this on the seam line as it is being positioned under the presser foot.

Narrow Seam **1** *First row of zigzag.* **2** *Second row of zigzag, seam trimmed close to stitching.* **3** *Seam edges neatened with a wider zigzag; lengths of thread still in position to prevent stretching.* **4** *Seam completed and pressed to one side.*

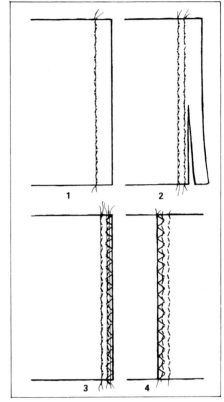

2 Hold this extra piece of thread along with your top and bobbin threads, to the back of the machine, and allow the zigzag stitch to work over the extra thread, which must be held taut for the length of the seam.

3 Repeat this for the second line of stitching and the neatening.

4 If the fabric has still stretched, pull up the extra thread to ease the seam back into shape before the final press.

> ### Machine setting
> *Presser foot:* Zigzag
> *Needle:* Ballpoint 90
> *Stitch width:* 1 for seaming, and 2–2½ for neatening
> *Stitch length:* 1½–2
>
> ### Requirements
> *Fabric:* Jersey-knit, 2 pieces – 30 cm
> (12″) × 15 cm (6″)
> *Tacking cotton*
> *Thread:* polyester

Edge Trimmed Seams **1** *Ric-rac machined into place 1.5 cm ($\frac{5}{8}$") from raw edge.* **2** *Seam tacked ready for machining using stitching where ric-rac attached as a guide.* **3** *Seam completed and pressed.*

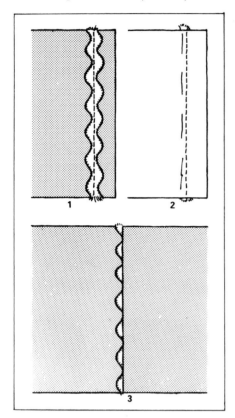

Placement of various trims all stitched on seam line.

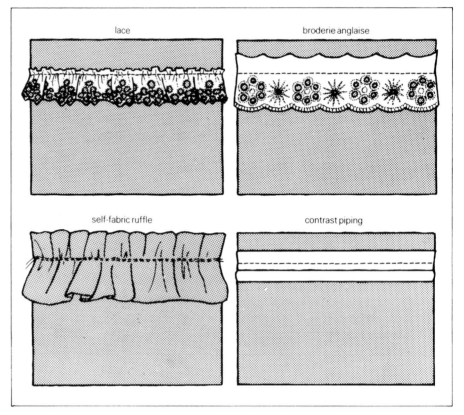

3a Edge Trimmed Seams

Inserting a trim to the edge of a collar, cuff, yoke or pocket gives a garment an air of distinction. Trimming straight seams can often emphasize the style of a garment. A trim to match one colour in a patterned fabric can make that colour more prominent. An inserted trim is between two layers of fabric, stitched on the seam line so that the correct amount of trim is visible from the right side. The following instructions are for ric-rac – a flat zigzag braid which gives a picot edge to a seam. Placement of lace, broderie anglaise, self-fabric frill and piping are shown in the diagrams above.

Machine setting

Presser foot: General
Needle: 80–90
Stitch width: 0
Stitch length: 2–2½

Requirements

Fabric: 2 pieces – 15 cm (6") × 7½ cm (3")
Ric-rac: 15 cm (6")
Tacking cotton
Thread

Instructions

1 Place the ric-rac on the RS of one of the pieces of fabric [along the 15 cm (6") side], so that the centre of the ric-rac is 1.5 cm ($\frac{5}{8}$") from the raw edge; tack and machine on this line.

2 Pin the RS of the second piece of fabric over the first, having raw edges even, and tack 1.5 cm ($\frac{5}{8}$") from the raw edge.

3 Turn your work over so that the machine stitching acts as a guide when sewing the pieces together.

4 Trim the fabric seam allowances, but not the ric-rac, and press seam open allowing the ric-rac to remain flat. (When the trim is on the edge of a collar, the seam allowances and edging would all be pressed together to the inside.)

3b Inserting Flat Lace Trim

This form of trimming has endless uses, and is really very easy to do. An insertion of lace down the front of a blouse, either side of the centre front, can often given an expensive look to an otherwise inexpensively made garment. Table-linen and bed-linen can also be enhanced with the simple insertion of straight-sided lace. Cushion covers too can be given this treatment and, if using an open see-through lace, a backing of ribbon in a contrasting colour can give quite a dramatic effect.

Instructions

1 Place the WS of the lace onto the RS of the fabric in the centre of the square, pin and tack.

2 Machine with a straight stitch near the edge of the lace on both edges.

3 Turn over the fabric and cut the fabric underneath the lace down the middle; press back the edges over each row of stitching on the WS.

4 Set your machine for zigzag and, with RS up, zigzag over the sides of the lace.

5 Trim away surplus fabric near the stitching on the WS.

Machine setting

Presser foot: General/Zigzag
Needle: 80–90
Stitch width: 0 for attaching lace, and 1½–2 for neatening
Stitch length: 2 for straight stitch, and 1½–2 for zigzag

Requirements

Fabric: Cotton – 15 cm (6") square
Lace: 15 cm (6") straight-sided, 5 cm (2") wide
Tacking cotton
Thread

4a Unlined Patch Pocket

Pockets can be both decorative and functional. There are several basic types and often a simple pocket in just the right place adds to the design of the garment. Children love pockets and like to use them, so make sure they are strongly made and firmly machined into place. A shaped unlined patch pocket (generally a top pocket on a shirt or blouse) is an easy one with which to start.

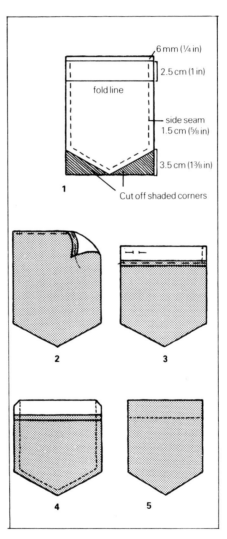

Machine setting

Presser foot: General
Needle: 80–90
Stitch width: 0
Stitch length: 2

Requirements

Fabric: Cotton – 13.5 cm (5¼") × 17.5 cm (7")
Tacking cotton
Thread

Instructions

1 Cut off the bottom corners as shown in the diagram.
2 Having the pocket RS up, turn 6 mm (¼") towards the WS at the top, tack and press.
3 Keeping the RS up, fold down 2.5 cm (1") for the hem, pin and tack.
4 Machine the sides, starting at the top of the fold [1.5 cm (⅝") from the raw edges] and continue right round the pocket to the top of the fold on the other side.
5 Trim the seam allowance to 6 mm (¼") and cut off the corners diagonally at the top of the pocket.
6 Turn the hem to the WS, roll seam between fingers and thumbs and tack. Continue turning the seam allowance to the WS, using the machine stitching as a measurement guide, pin, tack and press.
7 Machine stitch the hem in place, remove tacking press again. The pocket is now ready to be stitched to a garment.

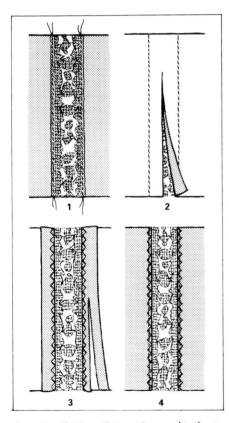

Inserting Flat Lace Trim **1** *Lace machined on to fabric.* **2** *Fabric cut on WS.* **3** *Edges pressed back over first lines of stitching and zigzagged down. Surplus fabric trimmed away.* **4** *Lace insertion completed.*

Unlined Patch Pocket **1** *Measurements of seam and top hem allowances.* **2** *Top edge turned and tacked.* **3** *Hem turned down on fold line.* **4** *Sides machined and seam allowance trimmed.* **5** *Hem machined in place, edges turned and pressed.*

Gently guide the fabric with light finger-tip control.

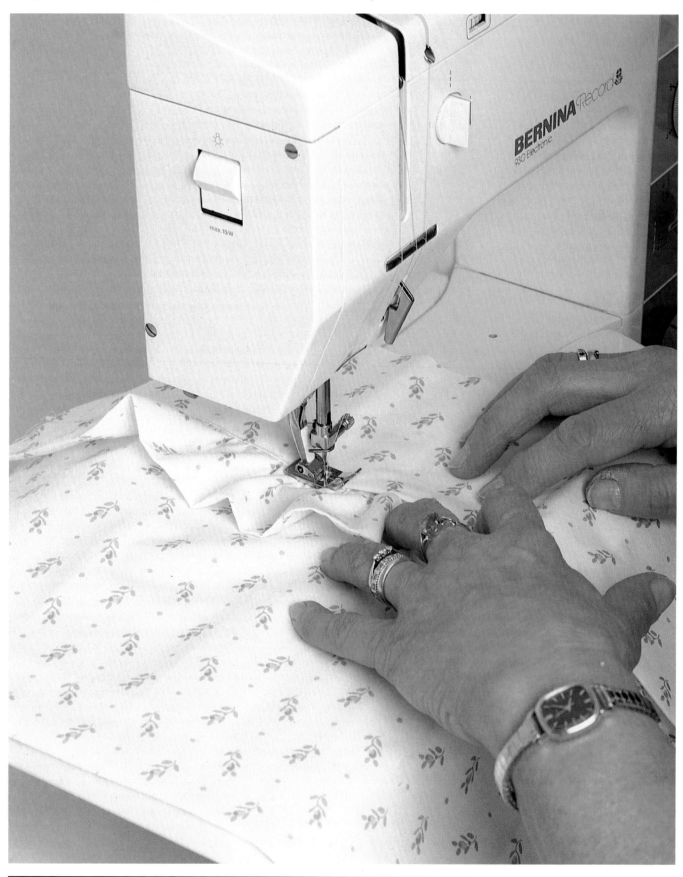

Lined Patch Pocket (Thicker fabrics) **1, 2** *Cut out.* **3** *Interfacing pressed into position.* **4** *Lining machined to pocket. Trim seam allowance; press towards lining.* **5** *Tacked ready for stitching.* **6** *Completed showing lining.*

4b Lined Patch Pocket

A lined square or oblong pocket is both simple and strong, which makes it ideal for children's wear, or for a pocket that is going to be used a lot. It can be made from one piece of fabric, thus eliminating a seam along the top, but this is only suitable in light/medium-weight fabrics. Thicker materials would be better with a thin lining fabric for the inside. The use of interfacing helps to retain the shape of a pocket.

Light/medium-weight fabrics with interfacing

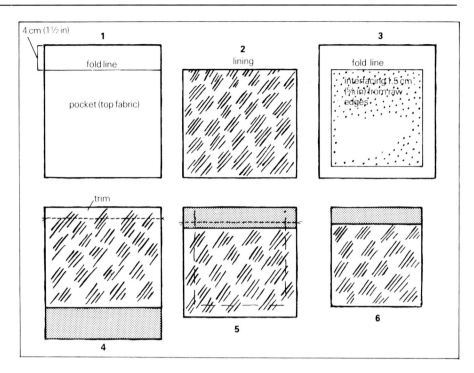

Machine setting

Presser foot: General
Needle: 80–90
Stitch width: 0
Stitch length: 2–2½

Requirements

Fabric: 28.5 cm (11¼″) × 16 cm (6¼″)
Interfacing: Light iron-on − 25.5 cm (10″) × 13 cm (5″)
Tacking cotton
Thread

Instructions

1 Press interfacing into position using a damp muslin and hot iron using an up-and-down action (refer to diagram for placement of interfacing).
2 Fold fabric in half with two RS together; then* tack and machine round from the fold (which is the top of the pocket), 1.5 cm (⅝″) from raw edges leaving a 5 cm (2″) opening on one side for turning through.
3 Trim seams to 6 mm (¼″), cut off the corners diagonally, turn the pocket through the 5 cm (2″) gap and slip stitch gap closed on the seam line.
4 Roll the edges of the pocket between fingers and thumbs, tack as you go.
5 Press well and remove tacking. The pocket is now ready to be top stitched to a garment.

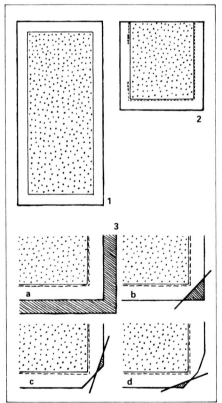

Lined Patch Pocket (Light/medium-weight fabrics) **1** *Placement of interfacing 1.5 cm (⅝″) from raw edges.* **2** *Pocket machined around, with reverse stitching either side of gap.* **3** *Trim seam allowance by cutting off the shaded part; follow steps a, b, c, d.*

Thicker fabrics with lightweight lining and interfacing

Machine setting

Presser foot: General
Needle: 80–90
Stitch width: 0
Stitch length: 2–2½

Requirements

Fabric: 18.5 cm (7¼″) × 16cm (6¼″)
Lining: 13.5 cm (5¼″) × 16 cm (6¼″)
Interfacing: Medium Iron-on 13 cm (5″) × 13 cm (5″)
Tacking cotton
Thread

Instructions

1 Press interfacing onto pocket piece using a damp muslin and hot iron (refer to diagram for placement of interfacing).
2 With RS together, join lining to pocket as shown; press turnings towards lining.
3 Fold pocket and lining RS together, on the fold line, having raw edges even.
4 Make up pocket following the previous instructions (**2***).

Now stitch the three pockets to a piece of fabric 45 cm (17¾″) × 25 cm (10″). This will enable you to practice pinning, tacking and top stitching pockets into position as you would on a garment.

Elastic Shirring 1 *First row of shirring worked. Diagram shows tacking guideline still in place.* **2** *Further rows of shirring worked.*

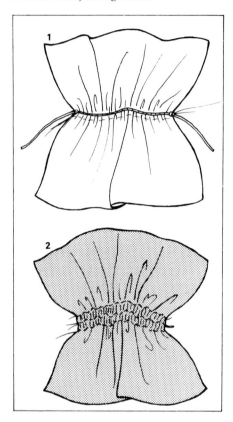

5a Elastic Shirring

Shirring is an effective method of controlling fullness. A child's skirt can be made from an oblong piece of fabric (instructions on page 61); sundresses and nightdresses too can all be made quite quickly. Two or three rows worked about 3 cm (1¼") from the neatened edge on the bottom of sleeves can give the effect of a frill. Shirring is always worked on single fabric before the seams are machined.

Machine setting

Presser foot: General
Needle: 80–90
Stitch width: 0
Stitch length: 4

Requirements

Fabric: Cotton – 30 cm (12") square
Shirring elastic
Thread

Instructions

1 Wind the shirring elastic onto the bobbin by hand, using very slight tension – not slack.

2 Mark a guideline on the fabric with tailor's chalk or tacking, 2.5 cm (1") from the raw edge.

3 Working with the RS up, presser foot edge against the marked line, sew the first row, leaving the ends of elastic and thread long enough to tie together at the back of the work.

4 The second and all subsequent rows are worked with the presser foot edge against the preceeding row of stitching. (**Note:** Remember to stretch the fabric to the original size as you work the rows of shirring – the more rows you work the stronger the elasticity will become.)

5 Knot elastic and thread ends securely.

5b Elasticated Waists

There are a number of patterns for dresses with elasticated waists, which means they will expand to pull over the shoulders, yet appear fitting to the waist once in position. Pattern instructions often state how to apply a casing, or how to make one from the waistline seam, ready to insert elastic, but on some silky type fabrics, this means that the gathers have to be arranged evenly everytime the garment is worn – to zigzag the elastic in place avoids this. It is easier to apply the elastic to the front and back of a garment separately, so that only a flat piece of fabric is dealt with as described below.

Instructions

1 Put a tack line in the centre of the fabric, as in the diagram. Fold fabric and elastic into two and mark the centre of each fold with a pin.

2 Place the elastic against the tack line and secure across the end with several zigzag stitches, stitch length at 0.

3 To sew the elastic in place, set stitch length to 2–2½, align elastic with the tacked guide and, with the centre of the elastic under the centre of the presser foot, work a few stitches with the handwheel.

4 With the needle out of the work, but with the presser foot down, hold the fabric and

Elasticated Waist 1 *Tack line for placement of elastic. Pins mark centres of fabric and elastic.* **2** *Elastic machined into place. Close zigzag stitches secure ends of elastic.*

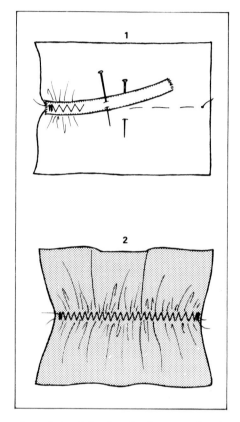

elastic behind the foot firmly in one hand, and at the same time stretch the elastic with the other hand and line up with marker pins; take hold of the fabric with the elastic and zigzag into place.

5 Just before you reach the pins, pause with the needle out and presser foot down, and remove the pins, holding the elastic and fabric both in front and behind the presser foot.

6 Continue machining to the end of the elastic and secure as at the start.

Machine setting

Presser foot: Zigzag
Needle: 80–90
Stitch width: 2½–3
Stitch length: 0 for securing elastic, and 2–2½ for stitching

Requirements

Fabric: Cotton – 30 cm (12") square
Elastic: 20 cm (8") approx. 6 mm (¼") wide
Tacking cotton
Thread

6a Narrow Single Turn Hem

Hems are the finishing touch to any garment, and there are many variations on how these are worked. They can be divided into three main categories: invisible, decorative and functional. The first one to practice is a narrow single-turn hem, suitable for flared skirts, where a deeper or double hem would restrict the swing of the style. It is the one to choose if you are working with a medium-weight fabric.

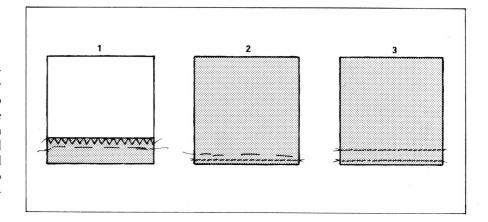

Machine setting

Presser foot: General/Zigzag
Needle: 80–90
Stitch width: 0 for straight stitch, and 2½–3 for zigzag
Stitch length: 2½–3 for straight stitch, and 2–2½ for zigzag

Requirements

Fabric: 25 cm (10″) × 15 cm (6″)
Tacking cotton
Thread

Instructions

1 Neaten the raw edge with zigzag; turn up 1.5 cm ($\frac{5}{8}$″), tack and press.
2 Machining from the RS edge stitch the fold.
3 Work a second row of stitching, having the side of the presser foot alongside the first row. Check after a few stitches that the stitch is at least 3 mm ($\frac{1}{8}$″) away from the neatened hem.
4 Press again.

Deep Single Turn Hem

A deep single turn hem is used a great deal when making garments in medium/ heavyweight materials. It is prepared by machine but catch stitched, by hand, invisibly into place. A row of machining using stitch length 4, is worked 6 mm ($\frac{1}{4}$″) away from the neatened edge, and if there is a slight flare the bobbin thread can be pulled up to make the hem lie flat against the garment.

Instructions

1 Neaten the raw edge with zigzag; using a long straight stitch, machine 6 mm ($\frac{1}{4}$″) from the neatened edge.
2 Turn up hem 4 cm (1½″), tack near the fold and press.
3 Then tack just below the straight stitch. Catch stitch into place by hand – have the fold and WS towards you and turn the edge back on the machine stitch line; this allows the hand stitching to be done below the neatened edge.

4 Fasten your thread into the hem and working from right to left if right-handed (reverse this if you are left-handed), take a thread or two from the garment and a little more along the hem on the machine line. (**Note:** Leave the thread loose.)
5 Press again but NOT over the neatened edge.

Machine setting

Presser foot: General/Zigzag
Needle: 80–90
Stitch width: 0 for straight stitch, and 2½–3 for zigzag
Stitch length: 4 for straight stitch, and 2½–3 for zigzag

Requirements

Fabric: 25 cm (10″) × 15 cm (6″)
Tacking cotton
Thread

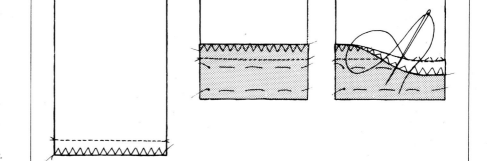

Deep Single Turn Hem **1** *Raw edge neatened and straight stitch worked 6 mm ($\frac{1}{4}$″) from the edge.* **2** *Hem tacked and pressed.* **3** *Catch stitch worked.*

Tablecloth with a double-turn hem, finished off by zigzagging crochet cotton over the machine stitch on the RS. See below and page 85.

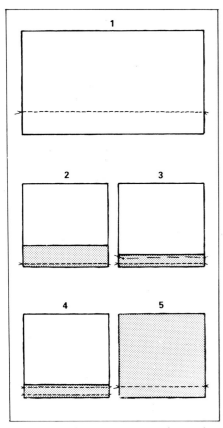

Narrow Double Turn Hem 1 *Machine stitch worked as a guide for hem depth.* **2** *Hem turned up and pressed.* **3** *Raw edge turned down inside hem and tacked.* **4** *Hem machined showing WS.* **5** *Finished hem showing RS.*

6b Narrow Double Turn Hem

This is a hem that is used for the bottoms of blouses and shirts, as it withstands constant washing. It is suitable for lightweight fabrics, thin cottons and blends of similar thickness. A narrow double turn hem can be worked round curves quite easily.

Machine setting

Presser foot: General
Needle: 80–90
Stitch width: 0
Stitch length: 2–2$\frac{1}{2}$

Requirements

Fabric: 25 cm (10″) × 15 cm (6″)
Tacking cotton
Thread

Instructions

1 Machine stitch just within 1.5 cm ($\frac{5}{8}$″) from the raw edge – as this is a guide for turning up the hem, it has to be worked accurately.
2 Turn up the hem so that the machine stitch will be just on the WS; tack, press and take out tacking.
3 Turn raw edge down inside the hem to the pressed fold line, tack and press. (**Note:** Pressing before machining helps to set the shape; also with the aid of a damp muslin, any fullness in a garment can be eased out before sewing.)
4 Edge stitch along upper fold and press again after machining.

Deep Double Turn Hem

A deep double turn hem can be used on garments made from cotton or cotton blends that are perfectly straight at the hemline; it is also one that is used on a lot of household items.

A better appearance is achieved if the hem has a complete double turn of fabric; this avoids a line showing on the RS that is generally visible when a narrow turn is followed by a wider turn of fabric. Used on a garment, it would be slip stitched into place, but for household items it would be machined.

Machine setting

Presser foot: General
Needle: 80–90
Stitch width: 0
Stitch length: 2–2$\frac{1}{2}$

Requirements

Fabric: 25 cm (10″) × 15 cm (6″)
Tacking cotton
Thread

Instructions

1 For a 5 cm (2″) deep hem, turn up 10 cm (4″), tack and press, remove tacking.
2 Turn raw edge down inside the hem to the fold line. Tack and press.
3 Machine (here you would slip stitch if making a garment) and press again.
(**Note:** For a deep double-turned hem on a fabric that can't be pressed, turn up and pin half the allowance, turn up again, tack, hem.)

Deep Double Turn Hem 1 *Full hem allowance turned up and pressed.* **2** *Raw edge placed to fold.* **3** *Hem machined into place.*

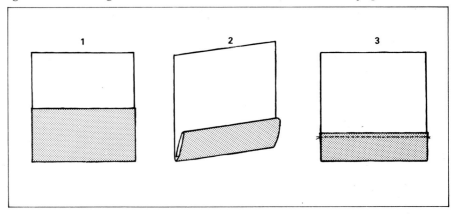

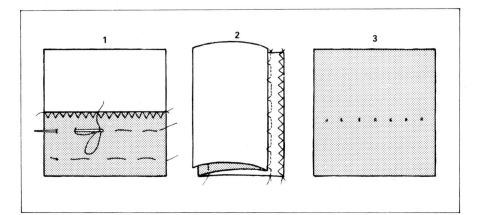

Blind Hemstitch Hem **1** *Hem turned, tacked, pressed and neatened.* **2** *Blind hemstitch worked* *with hem still in required folded position.* **3** *Finished hem showing RS.*

6c Blind Hemstitch Hem

The blind hemstitch is a machined hem using a pre-set stitch, which only leaves a dot of thread showing on the right side. With tweed fabric or a knitted ribbed jersey material, using a well-matched thread, it merges and so becomes invisible. It is really only suitable for a straight hem.

Machine setting

Presser feet: Zigzag and Blindstitch or attachment
Needle: 80–90
Needle position: centre for preparation; right for blindstitch (on some machines only)
Stitch width: $2\frac{1}{2}$
Stitch length: $2\frac{1}{2}$

Requirements

Fabric: Medium-weight tweed –
30 cm (12″) × 15 cm (6″)
Tacking cotton
Thread

Instructions

(**Note:** Check with your sewing-machine instruction book for this process.)

1 Turn a single 4 cm ($1\frac{1}{2}$″) hem, tack near the fold and press.
2 Neaten the raw edge with zigzag, and tack 1 cm ($\frac{3}{8}$″) from neatened edge.
3 Set your machine for blindstitch and attach foot. Place fabric under the foot, having the work folded so that three layers of fabric are to the left, leaving only the 6 mm ($\frac{1}{4}$″) single fabric to the right, as in diagram. (**Note:** The blindstitch consists of three straight stitches worked just to the right of the fold through single fabric and one zigzag stitch swinging to the left into the fold.)
4 At the start of machining, check that the needle just catches the fold. If it misses, increase stitch width a little; if it goes too far over, reduce the stitch width.

6d Bias Binding Hem

This is a decorative hem ideal for use on cotton garments, especially useful for letting down children's clothes, where it could be used on the right side in a contrast colour, with a second line of bias binding stitched over the fold mark of the original hem.

Instructions

1 Opening one fold out, place bias binding to raw edge of fabric, RS together. Machine into place, using a straight stitch and sewing along the fold crease of the binding.
2 Turn the binding to the WS, tack and press.
3 Work all further stitching with RS uppermost. Edge stitch the bottom, then work a second row approx. 1.3 cm ($\frac{1}{2}$″) from the first row to stitch down the bias binding. (**Note:** An easy way to ensure this, is to turn your work over to the wrong side and place it under the presser foot as though you were positioning to sew; then note which guideline on your needle plate the edge of the

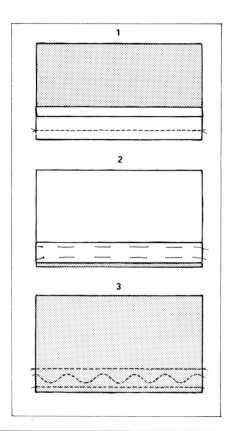

Bias Binding Hem **1** *Bias binding machined into place.* **2** *Bias binding tacked and pressed to WS.* **3** *Completed hem showing RS.*

Machine setting

Presser foot: General/Zigzag
Needle: 80–90
Stitch width: 0 for straight stitch, and 4 for decorative
Stitch length: 2 for straight stitch, and $1\frac{1}{2}$ for decorative

Requirements

Fabric: Cotton – 30 cm
(12″) × 15 cm (6″)
Bias Binding: narrow 30 cm (12″)
Tacking cotton
Thread

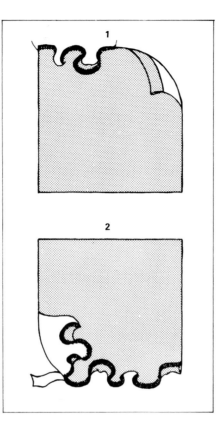

Lettuce Edge Hem 1 *Hem starting to be worked on RS.* **2** *Hem completed and surplus fabric being trimmed off close to stitching.*

hem rests against, when the needle would be sewing into the bias binding. However, remember to turn to the RS for the actual stitching.)

4 Finally, select a decorative stitch to be worked between the two rows of straight stitch. Set the stitch width and length for decorative sewing, and centralizing the presser foot between the two rows of stitching, work your chosen fancy stitch.

6e Lettuce Edge Hem

The Lettuce Edge hem is so called because the fluted effect resembles a lettuce leaf – it can only be achieved on a fine silky jersey fabric. It looks most attractive for evening wear, and can be worked using matching or contrasting thread to your fabric, depending on what effect you wish to achieve. It is a process that requires patient practice to become proficient, but once you have learnt the co-ordination of stretching the fabric at the same time as working a close zigzag, it really is quite easy.

Instructions

1 Turn a single 1.3 cm ($\frac{1}{2}$″) hem to the WS along the 30 cm (12″) edge, tack and press; take out tacking.

2 Position the work RS up so that the needle will go by the side of the fold on the right-hand swing and go into the two layers of fabric on the left-hand swing. Work the first few stitches using the hand wheel.

Machine setting

Presser foot: Zigzag
Needle: Ballpoint 80
Stitch width: $2\frac{1}{2}$–3
Stitch length: $\frac{1}{4}$–$\frac{1}{2}$

Requirements

Fabric: Fine, silky jersey – 30 cm (12″) widthways (stretchy) of fabric × 15 cm (6″) lengthways of fabric
Tacking cotton
Thread: Polyester

3 Pause with the needle out of the fabric and the presser foot down, then take hold of the fabric firmly behind the presser foot and about 10 cm (4″) in front. Stretching the fabric as much as you can, continue machining a close zigzag whilst allowing the fabric to move forward in its stretched state. (**Note:** Remember the more you stretch, the greater the effect of the fluted edge.)

4 When pausing to move the position of

your hands, always leave the needle up, otherwise you will bend or break it, and the presser foot down.

5 After completing the hem, trim off the surplus fabric close to the stitching.

PART THREE

Practice Plans for Further Processes 1–6

Knitting or sewing bag with decorative freehand machine quilting. See page 56.

The Practice Plans in Part Three are further processes used in dressmaking, with the exception of Decorative Sewing, which can be used for garments or household items. Fabric requirements are listed for each individual Practice Plan, and unless the type of fabric is specified, a firm, woven cotton is suitable. It would be an advantage to purchase 2–3 metres of material and 1–2 metres of interfacing to use, rather than obtain fabric for each process individually. Diagram patterns are given for some processes, which have to be drawn to full size on squared pattern paper. Some sewing magazines often print these, from which garments can be made, so it is as well to practice this procedure (instructions on p. 41).

When using these patterns, markings and symbols, such as dots and notches, have to be transferred from the pattern to the fabric; use a 'quick' method for this, such as a chalk pencil. There are several methods of marking in dressmaking and these are given in more detail in Part Four.

1a Neatening Slits – Faced Method

The bottom of long sleeves, when finished with a buttoned cuff, generally has a slit that requires neatening – the process is worked before the seams are machined. The faced method is the simplest and can be used for any fabric – it is certainly the most desirable one for thicker materials. This method can also be used for neatening a neck opening.

Machine setting

Presser foot: General/Zigzag
Needle: 80–90
Stitch width: 0 for straight stitch, and 2–3 for zigzag
Stitch length: 2–2½

Requirements

Fabric: 15 cm (6″) square, 9.5 cm (3¾″) × 6.5 cm (2½″)
Bondaweb: 2.5 cm (1″) × 7.5 cm (3″)
Tacking cotton
Thread

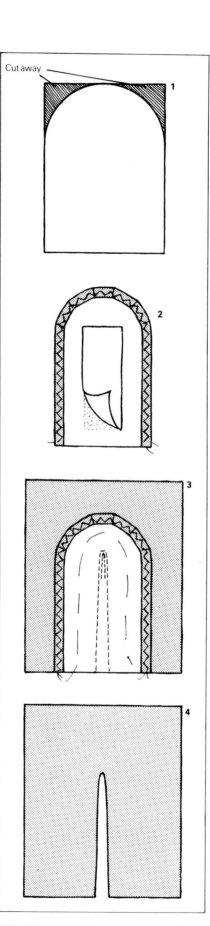

Cut away

Instructions

1 Cut off two corners to give a rounded shape to the facing rectangle (see diagram).
2 Turn under 3 mm (⅛″) on the sides and rounded end, tack and press before machining with a zigzag stitch, remove tacking.
3 Press the strip of Bondaweb down the middle of the facing, with the rough, adhesive side next to the WS of the facing, using a damp muslin and medium/hot iron; allow it to cool, before peeling off the paper backing.
4 Mark and tack a line 7 cm (2¾″) long, in the middle of a raw edge on the larger piece of fabric. Place the centre of the facing to the tacked line, with RS together; tack and machine as shown in the diagram, reinforcing the top with a second row of stitching, then remove tacking.
5 Slash between the stitching to the point, and turn facing to WS. Roll seam between fingers and thumbs, making sure the seam line is just to the WS on the last roll; tack as you go.
6 Press with a damp muslin and medium/hot iron. (**Note:** This will make the fabric adhesive bond the two layers, giving a crisp edge to the opening and will prevent any fraying at the top of the slash); remove tacking.
7 When using this method for medium to thick fabrics, do not turn under the edges of the facing for neatening, just zigzag the raw edges. On very thick materials use a matching lining for the facing, and use the first method of neatening.

Faced slit 1 *Using a round object as a guide, draw line to obtain curve shape.* **2** *Edge neatened; Bondaweb pressed into position; paper backing peeled off.* **3** *Facing tacked and machined.* **4** *Slash on centre line, then turn facing and press to the WS.*

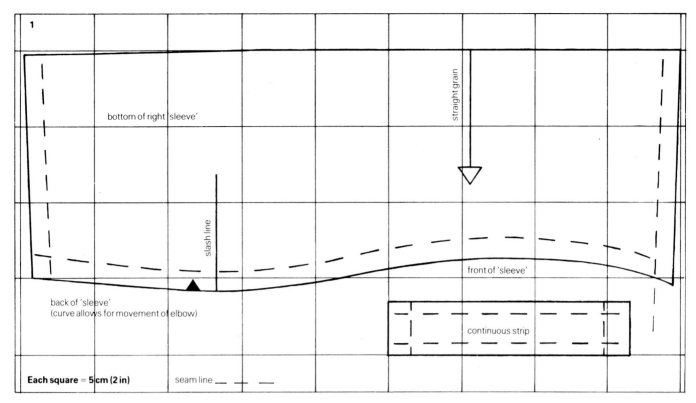

1

bottom of right 'sleeve'

straight grain

slash line

front of 'sleeve'

back of 'sleeve'
(curve allows for movement of elbow)

continuous strip

Each square = 5 cm (2 in)   seam line

Continuous strip *(Above)* **1** *By counting the squares on the grid in the diagram, mark the straight lines first on to the pattern paper; for curves mark dots following the shape and join them up. Fill in details required – balance marks, fold and straight grain lines, centre back and front, etc. – before cutting out the pattern. Cut out with single thickness fabric RS up, and place pattern as in diagram.*

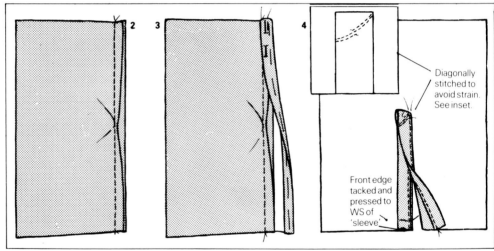

Diagonally stitched to avoid strain. See inset.

Front edge tacked and pressed to WS of 'sleeve'.

Continuous strip *(Above)* **2** *Strip machined into place RS uppermost.* **3** *Seam pressed towards strip; tacked edge pinned over machine stitching.* **4** *Front edge tacked and pressed to WS of 'sleeve'.*

1b Neatening Slits – Continuous Strip

The continuous strip method of neatening an opening on long sleeves is most useful on light to medium-weight fabrics; it is a strong method that withstands frequent washing. Working this process on the bottom of a 'sleeve' will enable you to use it again for Gathered Cuffs (p. 44).

Instructions

1 Make a pattern from the diagram using pattern paper, and cut out in fabric. Transfer markings to fabric, using a quick method with tailor's chalk (page 72), before removing the pattern.

Machine setting

Presser foot: General
Needle: 80–90
Stitch width: 0
Stitch length: 2–2$\frac{1}{2}$

Requirements

Fabric: 45 cm (17$\frac{3}{4}$") × 18 cm (7") for sleeve, and 16 cm (6$\frac{1}{4}$") × 3 cm (1$\frac{1}{4}$") for strip
Tacking cotton
Thread
Metric Pattern Paper

2 Slash opening on marked line, and place RS of strip to WS of sleeve. Working with the

(**Opposite**) *A selection of cushion covers – square cushions with piping, and appliqué and decorative quilting with ruffle; plain round cushions with ruffle and with piping. See pages 56, 89.*

Band opening (*Right*) **1** Note: *Top of band seam allowance is required when making the Easy Top (p. 66).* **2** *Place Fold-a-Band adhesive side down to cut to shape as shown; press to WS of facing.* **3** *Turnings tacked down the sides and pressed. To form a mitre follow steps a, b, c.* **4** *Facings tacked on CF line and stitching lines.* **5** *Facing stitched, cut and trimmed.* **6** *Under band edge-stitched, with the top band pulled through opening.* **7** *Top band edge-stitched to the dots.* **8** *Top band over under band and stitching completed.*

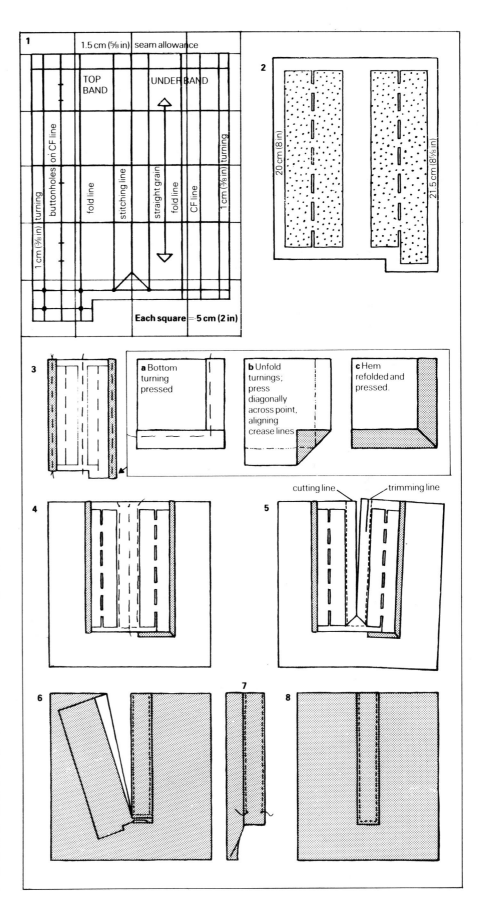

sleeve on top, machine, taking a 6 mm ($\frac{1}{4}''$) turning on the strip, but a graduated seam allowance on the sleeve – this is achieved by stretching the slash taut in a straight line which will create automatically a smaller seam at the top of the cut than at the start and finish. (**Note:** This is one process that is easier to accomplish by holding the strip in position rather than tacking it into place.)

3 Press the seam allowance towards the strip, turn under 6 mm ($\frac{1}{4}''$) on the other long side of the strip, pin and tack this over the first line of stitching.

4 Machine into place, remove tacking and press. (**Note:** To avoid strain at the top of the strip, stitch diagonally as shown in the diagram.)

5 Finally, tack and press the front edge of strip to inside.

1c Neatening Slits – Band Opening

The band opening can be used for sleeves or neck. It gives a professional look to a garment, but it requires the precise measuring of turnings, etc. to obtain a good result. It is well worth the time spent practicing this process to understand why this method needs exact preparation. The Practice Plan below gives the measurements of a facing for a neck opening. When used for sleeves the facing is somewhat smaller and a pattern piece is provided with commercial patterns.

Machine setting

Presser foot: General
Needle: 80–90
Stitch width: 0
Stitch length: 2–2½

Requirements

Fabric: 30 cm (12″) square, 25 cm
(10″) × 20 cm (8″)
Interfacing: Light Fold-a-Band 45 cm
(17¾″)
Tacking cotton
Thread
Metric Pattern Paper

When using this method, facings are applied to a neck edge before the band facing. For the bottom of sleeves, the opening is completed before the cuffs are applied.

Instructions

1 Make a pattern for the facing from the diagram using pattern paper. Cut out from the 25 cm (10″) × 20 cm (8″) piece of fabric, taking care to have your material RS up, and your pattern placed with the longer side to the left. Transfer all markings before removing the pattern.
2 Cut Fold-a-Band from the measurements in the diagram. Press into position, taking care that the edges are against the centre stitching lines, the slots on the fold line, and the outside edges against the turning allowance.
3 Tack and press turnings into position down the sides and the bottom of the longer side, mitring the corner of this (page 43).
4 Mark and tack a line in the middle of the raw edge on the square piece of fabric. Place the RS of the facing to the WS of the square, matching the CF line.
5 Tack and machine into place on the stitching lines, pivoting at the bottom corners; cut on CF line and diagonally to the corners; trim seams to 6 mm (¼″).
6 Turn the sample over and pull the under band through the cut, tack the attachment seam towards the band and press.
7 Fold band WS together on the slots. (**Note:** The turning that was pressed in the preparation stage should just cover the machine stitching.) Pin and tack to within 2.5 cm (1″) of the bottom.

8 Pull the top band right through the opening and this will allow the centre bottom seam to be tacked onto the RS, and press. The tacking at the bottom of the under band can now be completed, and can be tacked over the bottom seam through all layers.
9 Edge stitch both long edges of under band; take out tacking and press.
10 To finish the top band, tack the attachment seam towards the band. Fold on the slots and tack pressed edge over the machine stitching as before.
11 Edge stitch the long edges, finishing at the dots. Pull threads to the back of the top band and knot.
12 Lap top band over the under band, matching centre lines; tack and edge stitch through all layers, stitching from dot to dot, pivoting at each corner to complete the stitching. Pull threads to back, knot and thread them in invisibly.
13 Give a final press.

2a Gathered Cuffs

Gathering is a most effective way of controlling fullness, which gives movement and ease to a garment. Using the longest stitch on your sewing machine gives an even result very quickly. The thinner the fabric, the fuller the garment can be, but on thicker materials gathers tend to stick out if there is too much fullness.

Machine setting

Presser foot: General/Zigzag
Needle: 80–90
Stitch width: 0 for straight stitch, and 2–3 for zigzag
Stitch length: 2–2½ for stitching, and 4 for gathering

Requirements

Fabric: For cuff – 25 cm
(10″) × 14 cm (5½″) and sample used in (**1b**)
Interfacing: Ultrasoft light iron-on –
22 cm (8¾″) × 11 cm (4¼″)
Tacking cotton
Thread

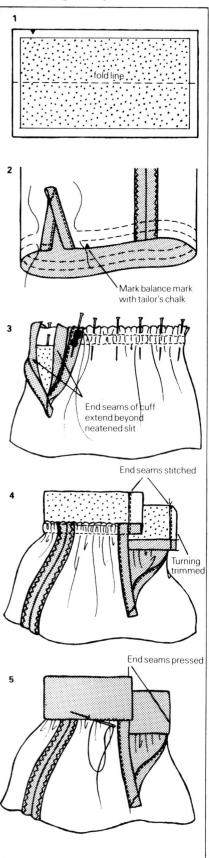

Gathered cuffs 1 *Interfacing pressed into place.* **2** *Two rows of gathering worked at the bottom of 'sleeve'.* **3** *Cuff pinned to 'sleeve'.* **4** *Seam trimmed to second row of gathering.* **5** *Cuff hemmed into machine stitching with tiny stitches.*

fold line

Mark balance mark with tailor's chalk

End seams of cuff extend beyond neatened slit

End seams stitched

Turning trimmed

End seams pressed

Instructions

1 Press interfacing to WS of cuff. Machine, neaten and press the 'sleeve' seam.

2 Set stitch length to 4 and with RS up, work two rows of gathering at the bottom of the sleeve, the first just within the seam allowance, the second 6 mm ($\frac{1}{4}$") away, nearer the raw edge.

3 Pull threads through to WS. Taking the measurement of the cuff (excluding the end seam allowances – in this sample, it is 22 cm [$8\frac{3}{4}$"]), pull the bobbin threads only, to gather to this measurement; secure threads at one end, figure-of-eight, onto a pin.

4 With the WS of the sleeve on the outside, place the cuff inside, matching notches and dots. With raw edges even, pin cuff to sleeve, arranging the gathers evenly. (**Note:** Place the pins from the raw edges inwards – this avoids the gathers being pushed along, as the pins will go across the gathering, rather than alongside.) Secure the threads onto a pin.

5 Tack and machine from the gathered side, making sure the gathers remain even, as they go through and under the presser foot. Trim seams up to the second row of gathering which remains in place, and press towards the cuff.

6 Tack and press 1.5 cm ($\frac{5}{8}$"), turning on the long edge of cuff. Folding the cuff on the fold line, RS together, tack and stitch end seams.

7 Trim to 6 mm ($\frac{1}{4}$"), cutting corners diagonally; turn to RS.

8 Roll seam between fingers and thumbs, tacking as you go; then press.

9 Hem stitch the turned edge to the machine stitch, and press again.

2b Gathered Waistband

Gathering the top of a skirt to apply a waistband is similar in method to the previous Practice Plan, but it is better to have a break in the gathering threads at the side seams of a skirt. A third row of gathering, placed 6 mm ($\frac{1}{4}$") below the first, helps to hold the seam line gathers more firmly – but as this gathering is taken out eventually, this method can only be done on fabric that will not be marked by the stitching. The sample to be worked simu-

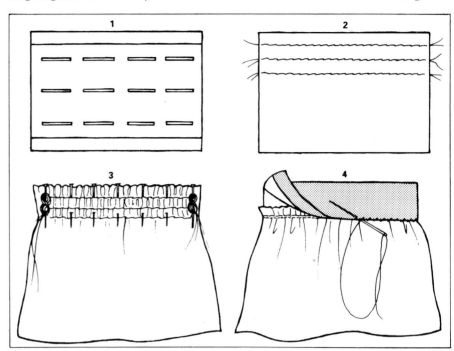

Gathered waistband **1** *Fold-a-Band pressed to 'waistband'.* **2** *Gathering threads machined in place using a large stitch.* **3** *Waistband pinned into position ready for tacking and machining.* **4** *Waistband hemmed into machine stitching.*

lates just a section of a 'skirt' and 'waistband'.

Instructions

1 Press Fold-a-Band to waistband, having the centre slots to the centre of the waistband.

2 Set stitch length to 4. With RS up, work three rows of gathering along the 40 cm ($15\frac{3}{4}$") length of fabric – the first line just within the seam allowance, the second and third 6 mm ($\frac{1}{4}$") away from the first, one above and one below.

3 Pull threads through to WS. Using the bobbin threads only, and pulling all three threads together, gather up to 20 cm (8") which is the measurement of the 'waistband'.

4 Placing RS of waistband to RS of gathered fabric with raw edges even, pin into position, placing pins from the raw edges inwards to avoid pushing the gathers along.

5 Tack with small stitches, making sure they are on a line with the slots in the Fold-a-Band, which will be on the waist seam line.

6 Machine from the gathered side; trim seam and press towards waistband.

7 Fold on centre slots, WS together; then fold on remaining slots and hem into machining.

8 Take out gathering thread below waistband, and press.

Machine setting

Presser foot: General
Needle: 80–90
Stitch width: 0
Stitch length: 2–2$\frac{1}{2}$ for stitching, and 4 for gathering

Requirements

Fabric: 40 cm ($15\frac{3}{4}$") × 25 cm (10"), and 20 cm (8") × 8"cm ($3\frac{1}{4}$")
Waistband interfacing: Firm Fold-a-Band – 20 cm (8") × 7 cm ($2\frac{3}{4}$")
Tacking cotton
Thread

3a Peter Pan Collar

A carefully made and well applied collar can 'make' a garment, as it is an important focal point and the first thing that is noticed. The Peter Pan type is the easiest to make because the shape of the collar at the neck is similar to the neck edge on the garment. It is used extensively on children's clothes, and ladies' blouses always look very feminine with this collar, especially if edged with lace.

Peter Pan collar *Make pattern (see p. 41). (Left)* 1 *Cut out (see p. 72) from double thickness fabric RS together. (Below)* 2 *Seam allowance trimmed and Vs cut out around edge.* 3 *Stay stitch around neck edge and cut snips towards stitching.* 4 *Collar pinned to neck edge with facings opened out.* 5 *Curve bias binding to fit neck edge. Hold binding firmly and stretch the fold edge.* 6 *Facings folded over collar, bias binding in position and tacked on seam line.* 7 *Collar finished.*

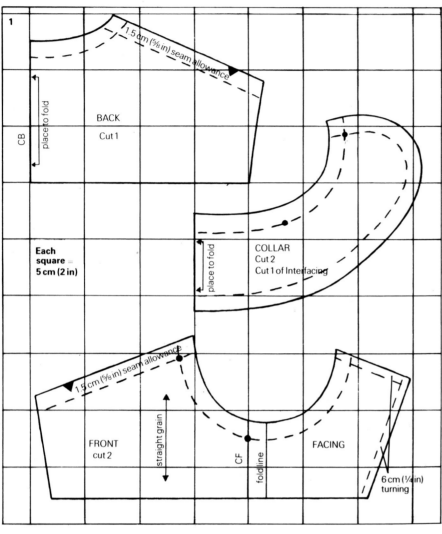

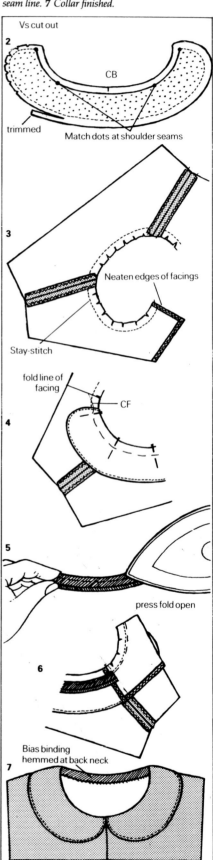

Instructions

1 Make pattern from diagram p. 41; cut out in fabric. Transfer markings from pattern to fabric, using a chalk pencil (page 72).

2 Cut interfacing for under collar, trim off seam allowance and press into position.

3 Place the two collar pieces RS together, tack and machine round, leaving neck edge open. Trim seam to 6 mm ($\frac{1}{4}$"), snip out Vs quite close together on the curves.

4 Turn to RS and, having the upper collar on top, roll seam edge between fingers and thumbs, making sure the seam goes just to the WS; tack as you go, press well.

5 Edge stitch round, having top collar uppermost; tack raw edges together.

6 Machine and neaten shoulder seams; turn under 6 mm ($\frac{1}{4}$") on shoulder and side edge of facings; tack and zigzag to neaten, press.

Machine setting

Presser foot: General/Zigzag
Needle: 80–90
Stitch width: 0
Stitch length: 2–2$\frac{1}{2}$

Requirements

Fabric: 114 cm (45") × 35 cm (14")
Interfacing: Ultrasoft light iron-on – 44 cm (17$\frac{1}{4}$") × 20 cm (8")
Bias Binding: Narrow 20 cm (8")
Tacking cotton
Thread
Metric Pattern Paper

Classic shirt using a purchased pattern. See page 76.

7 Stay-stitch, just within the seam allowance, round the complete neck edge and facings, having the facings opened out. Snip towards stitching – this allows the garment neck edge to open within the seam allowance.

8 Keeping the facings opened out, pin and tack collar to the RS of neck edge, matching centre back and dots. Fold facings over the collar and tack.

9 Shape bias binding into a curve.
Pin and tack the fold crease of the bias binding to the seam line of the back neck, allowing the binding to extend 1 cm (⅜″) over the facings.

10 Machine round complete neck edge taking 1.5 cm (⅝″) turnings. Trim down to 6 mm (¼″); snip collar towards stitching.

11 Turn facings RS out.

12 Pull collar away from the neck edge upwards, facings and bias strip downwards; tack round at neck edge and press seam only.

13 Tack and hem the folded edge of the bias binding at back neck edge, also facings to shoulder seams.

14 Press completely.

3b Revers Collar

An open-neck, turned-back collar and lapels called revers is one of the most comfortable to wear. The application is similar to a Peter Pan. Neatening of the back neck in this Practice Plan is with bias binding; but, when using a commercial pattern, if the garment has a yoke, this is generally self-lined in such a manner that it neatens the neck seam. With a more tailored garment there is often a shaped, back-neck facing.

Instructions

1 Make a pattern from the diagram and cut out in fabric. Transfer markings from pattern to fabric, using a chalk pencil (page 72).

2 Cut interfacing for under collar and facings, trim off seam allowance, press into position.

3 Place the two collar pieces RS together, tack and machine round, leaving neck edge open. Trim seam to 6 mm (¼″), cut corners diagonally and trim a little more off near the corners as shown in the diagram.

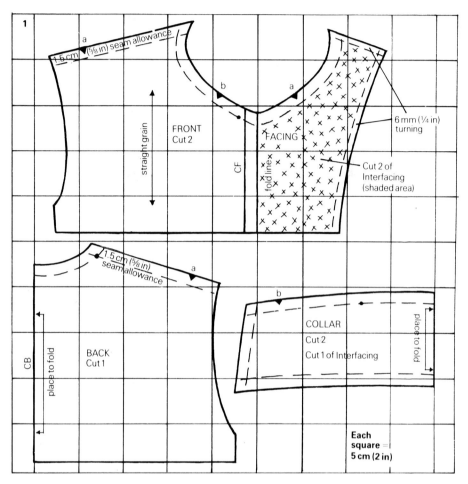

4 Turn to RS and, having the upper collar on top, roll seam edge between fingers and thumbs, making sure the seam goes just to the WS; tack as you go, press well, tack raw edges together.

5 Machine and neaten shoulder seams, turn under 6 mm (¼″) on shoulder and side edge of facings; zigzag to neaten.

6 Having the facings opened out, stay-stitch just within the seam allowance round the complete neck edge and facings. Snip towards stitching – this allows the garment neck edge to open up and match the convex shape of the collar.

7 Keeping the facings opened out and matching centre back, balance marks and dots; pin and tack the collar into position. Fold facings over the collar and tack.

8 Place curved bias binding along the back neck, having the fold crease to the seam line, and allowing the binding to extend 1 cm (⅜″) over the facings.

9 Tack and machine round the neck edge. Trim to 6 mm (¼″); snip collar towards stitching.

10 Turn facings RS out.

Machine setting

Presser foot: General/Zigzag
Needle: 80–90
Stitch width: 0
Stitch length: 2–2½

Requirements

Fabric: 114 cm (45″) × 50 cm (20″)
Interfacing: Ultrasoft light iron-on – 50 cm (20″) × 30 cm (12″)
Bias Binding: Narrow 20 cm (8″)
Tacking cotton
Thread
Metric Pattern Paper

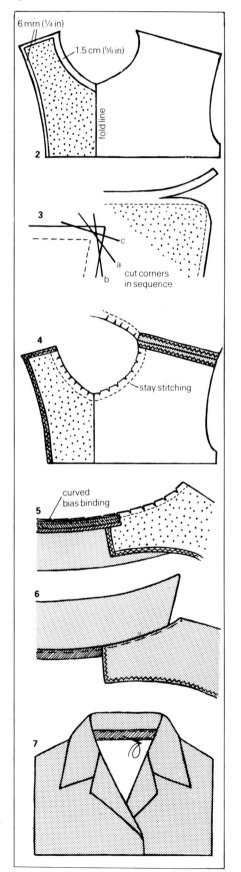

6 mm (¼ in)

1.5 cm (⅝ in)

fold line

2

3

c

a

b

cut corners
in sequence

4

stay stitching

curved
bias binding

5

6

7

Revers collar *Make pattern (see p. 41).* **1** *Cut out (see p. 72) from double thickness of fabric RS together.* **2** *Press fold line to use as guide for placement of interfacing.* **3** *Collar trimmed.* **4** *Stay-stitch around neck edge and cut snips towards stitching.* **5** *Collar machined to neck edge and seam trimmed (see p. 46).* **6** *Neck seam tacked for pressing.* **7** *Bias binding hemmed at back neck.*

11 Pull collar away from the neck seam upwards, facings and bias strip downwards; tack round, and press seam only with toe of iron.

12 Tack and hem the folded edge of bias binding into place, also facings to shoulder seams.

13 Press completely.

3c Shirt Collar

A shirt collar consists of a pointed collar, set into a neckband – it is this that allows a tie to be worn without distorting the actual turned-down collar. It is found on a lady's blouse as frequently as on an authentic gentleman's shirt, and is generally edge-stitched.

Machine setting

Presser foot: General
Needle: 80–90
Stitch width: 0
Stitch length: 2–2½

Requirements

Fabric: 114 cm (45″) × 35 cm (14″)
Interfacing: Ultrasoft light iron-on – 48 cm (19″) × 20 cm (8″)
Tacking cotton
Thread
Metric Pattern Paper

Instructions

1 Make a pattern from the diagram and cut out in fabric. Transfer markings from pattern to fabric, using a chalk pencil (page 72).

2 Cut out interfacing for under collar and one section of the collar band, trim off seam allowance and press into position.

3 With RS together, pin, tack and machine the pointed collar on the outer edges. Trim seam to 6 mm (¼″), cut corners diagonally and trim a little more off near the corners, as shown in the diagram.

4 Turn RS out and, having the upper collar on top, roll seam between fingers and thumbs, making sure the seam goes just to the WS; tack as you go, press well.

5 Tack raw edges together and edge stitch from RS.

6 Place and tack the interfaced collar band to the under collar, RS together, matching centre back, dots and balance marks. Turn under 1.5 cm (⅝″) on the neck edge of the second piece of the collar band and place this to the upper collar, RS together, raw edges even.

7 Machine round the curves and along the back of the collar band, sandwiching the collar; trim seam allowance to 6 mm (¼″), snip out small Vs from the curves and turn to RS.

8 Pulling the collar from the neckband, tack near the seam line, and press.

9 Machine and neaten shoulder seams; fold fronts to inside on lines shown on pattern and machine into place.

10 Stay-stitch neckline just within the seam allowance, and snip towards the stitching.

11 Position the RS of the under collar band to the RS of the neck edge and, matching all markings, pin, tack and machine.

12 Trim seam allowance to 6 mm (¼″), snip towards stitching, push seam into collar band, tack and press.

13 Hem upper collar band into machine stitching, and press; edge stitch band, and press again.

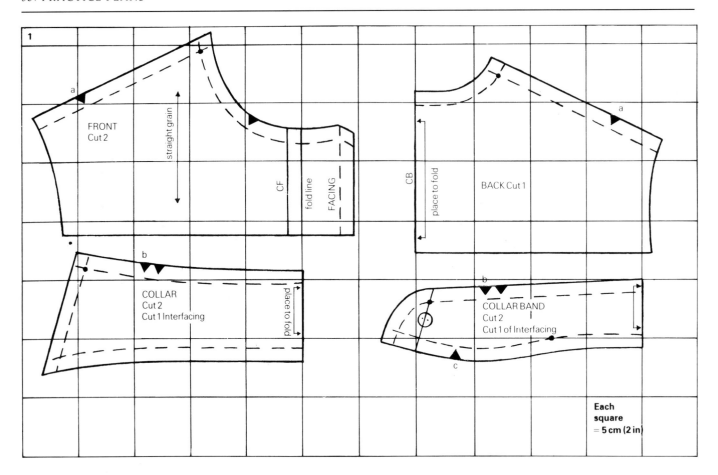

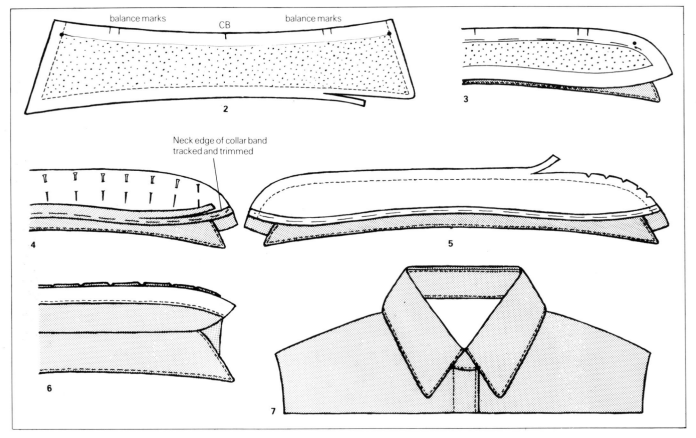

Shirt collar *Make pattern (see p. 41).* **1** *Diagram – cut out (see p. 72) from double thickness fabric RS together.* **2** *Collar machined and trimmed. Cut corners as in 3b (p. 49).* **3** *Interfaced collar band tacked to the collar matching all markings.* **4** *Collar band pinned in place sandwiching the collar.* **5** *Collar band machined to collar, seam trimmed, Vs cut out.* **6** *Collar band machined to neck edge of* 'shirt'. **7** *Completed collar, showing edge stitching on collar band.*

Machine-made buttonholes 1 *Marked and worked.* **2** *Pins placed.* **3** *Use button to mark guide lines for positioning. Work buttonholes between marked lines, 3 mm ($\frac{1}{8}''$) ease for thin fabrics, 6 mm ($\frac{1}{4}''$) for thicker.* **4** *Vertical buttonholes for shirts; buttons stitched to sit at top of buttonhole.*

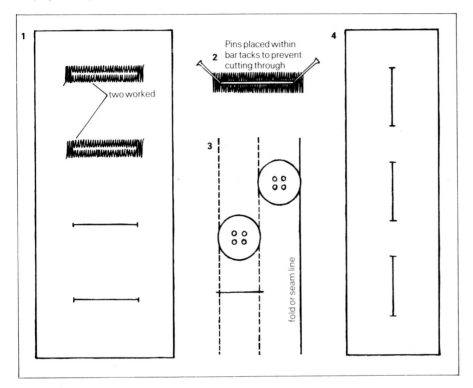

4a Machine-made Buttonholes

To achieve a good finish on a button-closing garment, it is essential to master the technique of making buttonholes. There are several ways of working them, and time spent practising is time well spent if you want to obtain a professional result. All zigzag sewing machines can produce a satin-stitch buttonhole, but they do vary in attachments and procedure, so it is better to refer to your own machine instruction book. Machine-made buttonholes are worked at the end of making a garment, and interfacing would already be in place where the buttonholes will be positioned. But before working them, press a small piece of Wundaweb between the top fabric and facing – this gives a firmer base for the machine needle to pierce, and also helps to prevent any tendency to fray when the buttonhole is cut. Always work each buttonhole towards the fold or seam line of the facing on a garment – this makes for strength where the button will finally sit.

Instructions

1 Fold fabric in half so you will be working through double thickness. (**Note:** Interfacing is not required at this stage of practising on a firm fabric such as calico.) Mark with a pencil, as in the diagram, and work several buttonholes.
2 To cut the buttonholes, put a pin at each end within the bar tacks (which are the wide zigzag stitches worked at each end), and slit with a seam unpicker – the pins will prevent cutting through the bar tacks. (Alternatively, start the slit with the unpicker in the centre of the buttonhole, then cut with small sharp scissors to each end.)

The diagram gives a guideline on the placement of buttonholes, and how much ease is required. A great deal depends on the thickness of the button and the fabric. (**Note:** When making a garment, always work a trial buttonhole on the fabric being used, with interfacing and Wundaweb in position, so that you can check the size of the buttonhole with the button.)

4b Piped Buttonholes

Piped buttonholes give a garment a tailored look and once you have become familiar with the different stages, they are not really difficult, although the smaller they are the more fiddly. It is best to practise them larger than life, then reduce them down to the required size. This type of buttonhole is suitable for medium/heavyweight fabrics, and this sample will give you an easy reference of piped buttonholes.

Machine setting
Presser foot: General
Needle: 80–90
Stitch width: 0
Stitch length: 2–2$\frac{1}{2}$

Requirements
Fabric: 30 cm (12") × 18 cm (7"), and 10 cm (4") × 18 cm (7"); 4 strips cut on straight grain – 23 cm (9") × 2.5 cm (1")
Bondaweb: 4 strips – 23 cm (9") × 2.5 cm (1")
Tacking cotton
Thread

Instructions

1 Mark fabric with two vertical lines, parallel with the 30 cm (12") side of the material using the tacking method, 5 cm (2") in from each side, and five horizontal lines spaced at 5 cm (2") apart.
2 Prepare piping strips by pressing on Bondaweb with a damp muslin and medium/hot iron; allow to cool and peel off

Machine setting
Presser foot: Buttonhole
Needle: 80–90
Stitch width: 1$\frac{1}{2}$–2 or automatically connected on some machines
Stitch length: Nearly 0

Requirements
Fabric: Calico – 15 cm (6") square
Thread: Polyester

Piped buttonholes 1 *Positioning for tacking guide lines.* **2** *Bondaweb pressed onto piping strip, backing removed.* **3** *Piping tacked into place.* **4** *Piping strips machined into place.* **5** *Cutting lines shown from WS.* **6** *Folded edges tacked together; strips tacked down along each side; piping pushed through cut.* **7** *Vs machined to piping strips; strips trimmed.* **8** *Buttonhole cut through; raw edges turned, hemmed.*

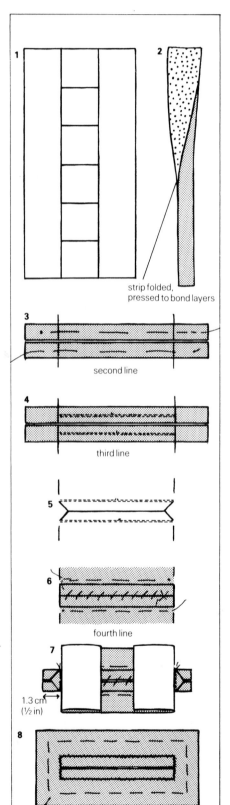

strip folded, pressed to bond layers

3

second line

4

third line

5

6

fourth line

7

1.3 cm (½ in)

8

facing tacked in place   fifth line

the paper backing. Fold strip in half lengthwise, WS together, having raw edges even and press again; the two layers will bond together. Cut each strip in two.

3 Place two pieces of piping to the second horizontal line, with the cut edges meeting; tack in place. Mark vertical lines over the piping strips using a ruler and tailor's chalk; then repeat this on the third marked buttonhole.

4 Machine both pieces of piping into place along the middle of the piping, starting in the centre and going to one side, then to the other, and back to the centre. (Using this method, there is no chance of the machining coming undone.) To ensure straight stitching, pivot your work round, with the machine needle in the fabric, when you reach the vertical line each time.

5 Cut fabric at the back of the piping along the marked line to make the buttonhole, taking care not to snip the piping – a straight cut in the middle for 5 cm (2″), turn to WS and then cut diagonally to the corners, this time taking care not to cut the stitching.

6 Proceed to the fourth marked line and, after working the buttonhole to the cutting stage, post the piping through to the back, and tack the fold edges together by oversewing. Tack along each side of the buttonhole for the length of the machining, making sure the Vs are to the back; these can now be machined to the piping strips as shown in the diagram. Press on WS having a thick cloth underneath, and a damp muslin on top.

7 Work the process right through on the fifth line; then using the 10 cm (4″) × 18 cm (7″) piece of fabric for a facing, pin and tack to the back of the buttonhole, having WS together.

8 Remove tackings that are keeping the buttonhole closed and cut the facing in the same way as the buttonhole, turn in raw edges and hem into place.

Note: When you require to work this type of buttonhole on a garment, prepare your strips as above, but trim the width of the piping to 6 mm (¼″) before using. Practice several buttonholes the size required in the material of your garment.

4c Rouleau Loops

Rouleau can be used in various ways and one of them is for buttonloops. It is very often the choice for special occasion outfits, especially when used with covered buttons; like the loops, they are made from the fabric of the garment. Strips are cut on the bias to make rouleau from woven material, but when working with a knitted fabric, cut the strips on the lengthwise grain. If jersey-type material was cut on the bias, it would have too much stretch.

Machine setting

Presser foot: General/Zigzag
Needle: 80–90
Stitch width: 0 for straight stitch, and ½ for zigzag
Stitch length: 2–2½ for straight stitch, and 1½–2 for zigzag

Requirements

Fabric: 2 pieces – 15 cm (6″) × 10 cm (4″)
Bias strip: 30 cm (12″) × 2 cm (¾″)
Rouleau turner or large-eyed, blunt-pointed wool needle
Tacking cotton
Thread

Instructions

1 Fold bias strip, RS together, in half lengthwise and machine down the centre, with zigzag stitch, slightly stretching the strip as you go. Leave the turnings on as they will 'fill' the rouleau to give a rounded appearance when finished.

2 Push the rouleau turner or wool needle into the tube and firmly sew the eye to one layer of fabric, and ease the end over the eye of the turner or needle; then pushing the fabric to ruche over the turner, pull the rouleau over the eye; repeat this until it is completely turned through (see diagram).

3 Cut stitching to release the turner (DO NOT PRESS); and cut rouleau into 5 cm (2″) pieces.

4 Make a template to position the loops, from the diagram, using greaseproof or thin paper; tack this to the RS of one of the pieces

Rouleau loops **1** *Eye of turner sewn to machined bias strip.* **2** *Strip being turned.* **3** *Turned RS out.* **4** *Template for positioning loops.* **5** *Button loops* *tacked and machined into place with template still in position.* **6** *Sample completed with facing turned to WS and seam line pressed.*

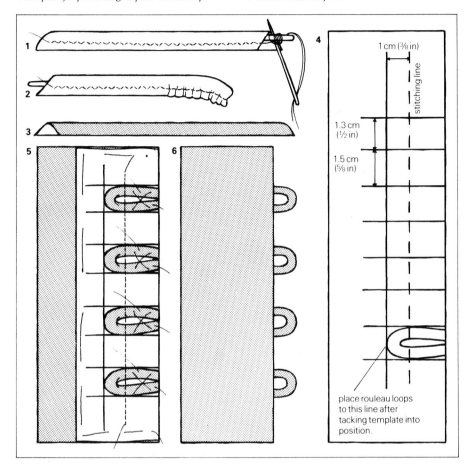

of fabric. Tack the loops into position and machine on seam line; remove tacking and tear away the paper.

5 Place the second piece of fabric over the loops, RS together, and tack. Turn your sample over and machine into place, following your first stitching.

6 Take tacking out and trim seam allowance to 6 mm ($\frac{1}{4}$″). Roll the seam between fingers and thumbs, and tack as you go; press the seam line only.

5a Overlap Zip

Sooner or later you will be making a garment that requires a zip. Most fitted garments require this form of fastening, and once you have learnt the correct way to work this process, you will not avoid the garments that do require one. The Practice Plan below is worked as for a left side opening in a lady's skirt.

Instructions

1 Place the two pieces of fabric, RS together, and using the 30 cm (12″) mea-

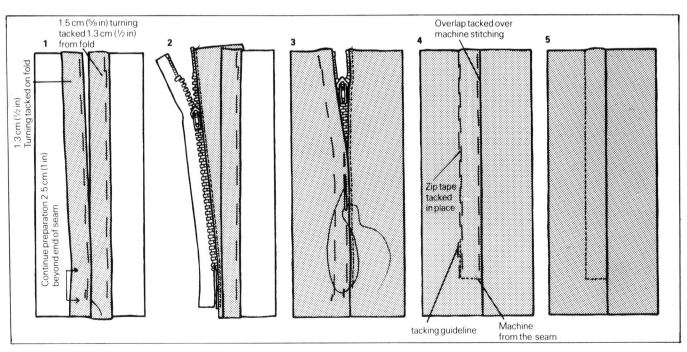

Overlap zip **1** *Turning tacked. Continue preparation.* **2** *Underside fold against zip teeth and machined into place.* **3** *Fold of overlap tacked over* *machine stitching.* **4** *Machine from seam.* **5** *Completed.*

Cushion cover with appliqué and piping. See page 89.

Centred zip 1 *Centre seam – zip opening machined.* **2** *Guide lines.* **3a** *Zip positioned for tacking.* **3b** *Tacking.* **4** *Completed.*

Machine setting

Presser feet: General and Zipper
Needle: 80–90
Stitch width: 0
Stitch length: 2–2½

Requirements

Fabric: 2 pieces – 30 cm
(12″) × 15 cm (6″) in medium weight
cotton or wool
Zip: 18 cm (7″)
Tacking cotton
Thread

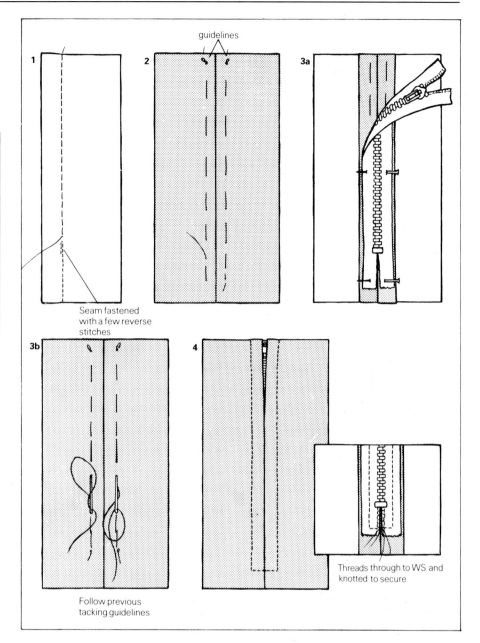

surement for the seam, machine 1.5 cm (⅝″) from the raw edges for 9 cm (3½″); press seam open.

2 Having the WS towards you and the opening to the top, turn 1.5 cm (⅝″) on the RH side and tack 1.3 cm (½″) from the fold – this will be your guide line for stitching in the zip, so be very accurate with the measurement for your tacking.

3 On the other side, which is the underside, turn 1.3 cm (½″) and tack near to the fold – be sure to continue the preparation for this side 2.5 cm (1″) below the end of the seam. Press well, taking care not to stretch the fold edges.

4 Place the closed zip with the slide tag 3 cm (1¼″) below the top of your sample and, with the teeth against the underside fold, tack the entire length of the zip tape. Fix the zipper foot into position, according to the instructions in your machine manual.

5 With RS up, stitch the zip into place, starting at the very bottom of the tape, working towards the top, pausing with the needle in your work 7.5 cm (3″) from the top. Lift the presser foot to enable you to open the zip, take the slide tag past the needle, lower the presser foot, and machine to the top. Take out the tacking.

6 Working from the RS, tack the fold of the overlap so that it just covers the machine stitching of the underside. Tack the zip tape into position on the line of your preparation tacking.

7 Still working from the RS and starting from the seam at the bottom of the zip, machine at right angles for 1.3 cm (½″), making sure you stitch through the very bottom of the zip tape. Leaving your needle

in the down position, pivot round and continue sewing on your tack guide line, stopping 9.5 cm (3″) from the top, again with the needle in your work.

8 Lift presser foot, take out the tacking that is keeping the opening closed, pull the zip slide tag down past the needle, lower the presser foot and continue stitching to the top. Take out all tacking.

9 Press along the stitching line, using the toe of the iron and having a damp muslin in place, taking care not to go over the zip teeth.

If you are putting in a zip for a back opening, the right hand side goes over the left. The positioning of the zip, 3 cm (1¼″) below the raw edges of a garment, enables either a waistband or facing to be machined into place without going too near the pull tag of a zip – if it was nearer it would cause a bulge.

5b Centred Zip

When inserting a zip fastener in a centre front opening of a dress, the lines of stitching must be equal distances from the centre – this also applies when using open-ended zips for anoraks or jackets.

Instructions

1 Place the two pieces of fabric, RS together, and using the 30 cm (12″) measurement for the seam, machine 1.5 cm (⅝″) from the raw edge for 9 cm (3½″); fasten thread by reversing for a few stitches.

2 Alter stitch length to 4, and machine the remaining 21 cm (8½″) keeping the same distance from the raw edges. Press complete seam open.

3 Tack guide lines 6 mm (¼″) from the seam

English quilting 1 *Tack three layers together,
always working from centre outwards.*
2 *Freehand quilting.* 3 *Diagonal quilting.*
4 *Completed.*

Machine setting

Presser feet: General and Zipper
Needle: 80–90
Stitch width: 0
Stitch length: 2–2½ (4 for temporary
seam stitching)

Requirements

Fabric: 2 pieces – 30 cm
(12″) × 15 cm (6″) in medium weight
cotton or woven wool
Zip: 18 cm (7″)
Tacking cotton
Thread

6a Decorative Sewing – English Quilting

There are many uses for English Quilting
which is a decorative way of sewing
together three layers of fabric, the middle
one being terylene wadding, which is the
easiest to use and is available in various
thicknesses. A quilted yoke, cuffs and/or
pockets can make a garment feel and look
special; also there are many household items
that can be made by using quilting. When
preparing quilting for use on a garment,
make up a piece larger in size than the
pattern and cut to shape afterwards.

Machine setting

Presser foot: Quilting plus guide (if
your machine is not supplied with
quilting accessories, an embroidery
or zipper foot can be used)
Needle: 80–90
Stitch width: 0
Stitch length: 3–4

Requirements

Fabric: 30 cm (12″) squares of
closely woven cotton
Wadding: Lightweight terylene
Lining: Thin cotton
Tacking cotton
Thread

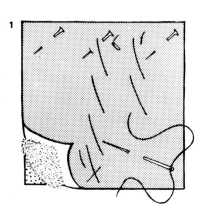

Start and finish at centre

1a shows first across line of stitching
working from centre

stitching lines numbered in order of
working

Edges zigzagged to neaten

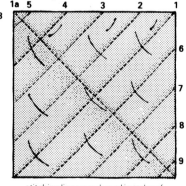

on both sides, using small stitches. Place the
RS of the closed zip to the wrong side of
your sample, centralizing the teeth to the
centre seam line, having the slide tag 3 cm
(1¼″) below the top of your fabric. Place a
couple of pins in to hold the zip whilst
tacking. Thread two needles with tacking
cotton so that both sides of the zip can be
tacked, step-by-step – this stops the zip
straying from the centre line.
4 Start on one side at the bottom and work
a couple of tacking stitches; then with the
second needle work two stitches on the
other side; alternating between the two
sides, tack in this manner to the top.
5 Fit the zipper foot into position. With the
RS up, starting from the seam at the bottom
of the zip, and well below the zip stop end
but catching in the tape, machine across at
right angles to the seam for 6 mm (¼″),
pivoting round with the needle in the fabric,
releasing the presser foot to do so.
6 Continue machining on your first tack
guide line, pausing 7.5 cm (3″) from the top
of your work with needle in the fabric. Lift
the presser foot, take out the large machine
stitch that is keeping the opening closed to
enable you to open the zip, lower presser
foot and complete the stitching.
7 Work the second side in the same
direction in a similar manner.
8 Take out the remaining machine stitching down the centre, and all tacking.
9 Press along the stitching line, using the
toe of the iron and having a damp muslin in
place, taking care not to go over the zip
teeth.

Instructions

PREPARATION

1 Place lining RS down on a flat surface,
cover with the wadding, and the top fabric,
RS uppermost.
2 Place two or three pins to hold the layers
together ready for tacking, which is worked
from the centre outwards; DO NOT pull the
tacking thread tight.

FREEHAND QUILTING This is by far the
easiest, but still very effective.
1 Start machining somewhere near the
centre and wend a pathway with your
stitching, turning your work gradually with
a light touch, this way and that, sewing at a
steady pace, ending where you began.

2 Take the threads through to the WS and knot. Remove the tacking.

DIAGONAL QUILTING

1 Prepare another square, following the preparation instructions above.

2 Draw a line diagonally from corner to corner with a ruler and tailor's chalk; follow this line for the first row of machining.

3 Fix and set the quilting bar 2.5 cm (1″) from the needle and having this guide against your first row of stitching, machine the second row.

4 Continue working more rows to the corner, having the guide against each preceeding row.

5 Fix the quilting bar to the other side of the presser foot and set it at the same distance from the needle as before. Work from the centre to the corner again, machining further rows of stitching in the same direction.

6 Now work across the rows of stitching, marking and starting from the centre as before. Remove all tacking.

Note: Another square could be worked using the same principle, but with the lines of stitching parallel to the sides of the fabric, thus forming squares.

If you haven't a quilting bar, measured lines for stitching must be marked, either by tailor's chalk or tacking. Quilting does not require pressing.

6b Decorative Sewing – Appliqué

Appliqué is a form of embroidery with fabrics. Flowers can be cut from a printed fabric and applied to a plain material, the outlines are machined with a zigzag stitch, and very effective results can be achieved. Children like their 'in' characters appliquéd to garments or things they use, and these can easily be traced from their reading or painting books.

Instructions

1 Press interfacing to WS of the cotton square.

2 Draw or trace shapes onto the paper side of Bondaweb, leaving spaces in between, e.g. the flower head and leaves. Trace the

Appliqué **1** *Shapes traced on to paper side of Bondaweb.* **2** *Flowerhead and leaves pressed in place on an interfaced cotton square.* **3** *Flower centre ready for cutting out.* **4** *Completed.*

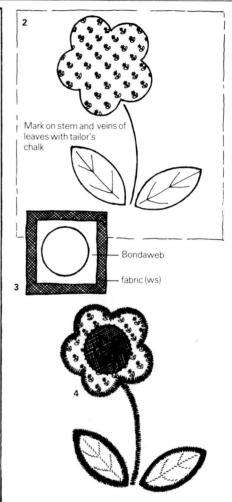

centre of the flower separately too, as this will be worked in a different colour/fabric.

3 Cut the Bondaweb, leaving a margin round your tracings. Press these onto the WS of contrasting fabric (having the paper side of the Bondaweb uppermost), using a damp muslin and an iron set at the correct temperature for the material being used. Allow to cool, cut out the shapes and peel off the paper.

4 Position, adhesive side down, and press into place on the RS of the cotton square, using the same pressing procedure as before. Zigzag round the shapes, pull top threads through to the back and knot.

5 Close your zigzag up a little for working the veins of the leaves, marking these lightly with tailor's chalk to give a guide line.

6 Set your machine for a close satin stitch for the stems, which again can be marked in with tailor's chalk. (**Note:** Refer to Practice Plan **1b** in Part Two for zigzag instructions).

7 Press work on WS.

Machine setting

Presser foot: Embroidery or zigzag
Needle: 80–90
Stitch width: $1\frac{1}{2}$–2
Stitch length: $\frac{1}{4}$–$\frac{1}{2}$ for working round flowers; nearly 0 for stems

Requirements

Fabric: 30 cm (12″) square of cotton
Interfacing: Ultrasoft light iron-on – 30 cm (12″) square
Bondaweb: Sufficient for appliqué
Odd pieces of fabric
Thread: Matching or contrasting with the appliqué

PART FOUR

Making
Garments

Quickie skirt and easy top. See pages 64, 66.

Descriptive fabric terms

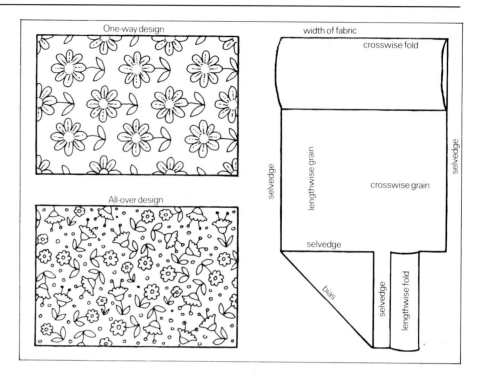

A great sense of achievement is felt when, in the early days of learning to sew, easy garments are made, and often the simple ones are very effective. A child's skirt made from an oblong piece of fabric, shirred at the waist before the seam is closed, uses the processes already practised, and a matching bolero can be made using your new skills. A lady's skirt from measurements, and a sleeveless blouse from a diagram, make a complete outfit. These are all suitable for a beginner to start making garments.

Choosing Fabrics

Fabric is made in several widths. Those commonly available are: 90 cm (36″), 115 cm (45″), 140 cm (54″), and 150 cm (60″). Thin lightweight fabric is often on rolls, medium/heavyweight material is generally folded, then wrapped round a flat piece of board.

The newcomer to sewing would be wise to choose a cotton or a blend of cotton/polyester, with a higher percentage of cotton to polyester, or at least a 50/50 combination. All are made in light, medium and heavyweight, which makes this type of material suitable for many garments.

Another easy-to-handle fabric, which sews and presses well, is firmly woven wool, or wool blended with a low percentage of man-made fibres. Blends with a high percentage of synthetic fibres, and many of the 100% man-made materials are very springy and therefore more difficult to handle, which is a very good reason to avoid them at first!

For the beginner a plain woven or all-over design fabric is the most suitable. Checks, plaids, stripes and diagonal prints should be avoided. They are for the more advanced dressmaker, needing extra time on cutting out, preparing and sewing, which could be very off-putting to anyone learning to sew. It is far better to master sewing processes, and become familiar with your sewing machine by working with easy materials, before progressing to more advanced techniques.

Descriptive Fabric Terms

Phraseology describing fabric often bewilders, and it is absolutely essential that the meaning of certain phrases, such as 'With Nap', 'Without Nap', 'One-Way Design', and 'All-Over Design', and so on, are understood.

With Nap is fabric with a nap or pile (raised surface) that feels smoother when stroked in one direction rather than the other – velvet is a good example; it also appears a shade lighter in one direction and darker in the other. Shading also applies to jersey and all knitted materials. Drape these fabrics on the body and look in a mirror to see which gives the best appearance – it is the deeper shade that is the richer.

Without Nap is a woven fabric without any raised surface. It feels smooth whichever way you stroke it and looks the same when viewed from different directions.

One-Way Design is a printed or woven design that only looks correct when viewed from one way, e.g. flower heads with stalks, which are printed with the stalks all one side of the flower head.

All-Over Design is a printed or woven design, that does not have a top and bottom to it – it appears exactly the same in both directions. Fabric has to be assessed at the time of purchasing, as a little more is required if it has a nap, pile, shading or one-way design, because the garment or item has to be cut out with the pattern pieces all pointing in the same direction.

Selvedge is a narrow, tightly-woven edge on the lengthwise grain of fabric. It prevents the material from fraying, and should not be used within the construction of a garment as it has a tendency to pucker.

Lengthwise Grain are the warp threads which run the length of the fabric parallel to the selvedge. These are generally the strongest threads in woven material.

Crosswise Grain are the weft threads that weave under and over the warp threads at right angles.

Bias is on the diagonal fold between the lengthwise and crosswise grains – this gives maximum stretch in woven materials. Fold fabric at 45° to the selvedge to obtain this, when instructions are given to 'cut bias strips'.

Preparing Fabric for Cutting Out

Press fabric on the wrong side to smooth away creases. A steam iron can be used for cotton or cotton blends, but for wool and wool mixtures use a damp muslin and dry iron. Make sure you press evenly and over the entire length of material, keeping the movement of the iron with the lengthwise grain of the fabric and with an up-and-down action. Press out the fold line, if there is one. Allow the fabric to cool and dry before pinning the pattern into position and cutting out.

Child's Skirt and Bolero

(FROM MEASUREMENTS AND DIAGRAM PATTERN)

Children like clothes that enable them to dress themselves, so the skirt especially will be enjoyed. It requires a small remnant and only a little time to sew. The matching bolero turns it into an outfit when worn with a T-shirt.

Skirt

Work out fabric requirements for the skirt by measuring waist and length required. Approximately twice the waist measurement is required for shirring. Add 7.5 cm (3″) to the length measurement for the hem and top of skirt. Generally, a strip across the 90 cm (36″) width fabric is sufficient for the small size, and 115 cm (45″) width will be adequate for the larger one.

Machine setting

Presser feet: General/Zigzag and Quilting
Needle: 90
Stitch width: 0, for straight stitch, and 3–4 for zigzag
Stitch length: 2–2½ for seaming, 3–4 for quilting, and 2–3 for zigzag

Requirements

Fabric: Width 90 cm (36″) – Size 2–3: skirt length + 30 cm (12″) for bolero; width 115 cm (45″) – Size 4–5: skirt length + 30 cm (12″) for bolero
Wadding: 40 cm (16″) × 30 cm (12″)
Lining: Thin cotton – 40 cm (16″) × 30 cm (12″)
Bias binding: 2.5 cm (1″) wide
Shirring elastic
Tacking cotton
Thread
Metric pattern paper

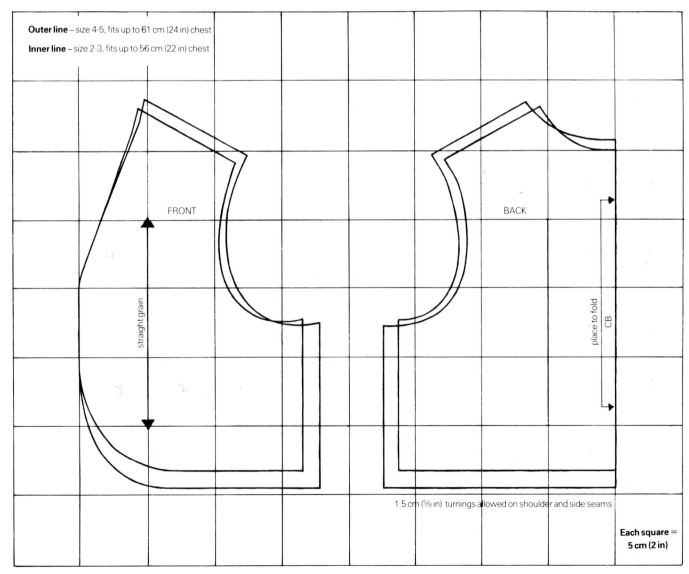

Outer line – size 4-5, fits up to 61 cm (24 in) chest
Inner line – size 2-3, fits up to 56 cm (22 in) chest

FRONT

straight grain

BACK

place to fold

CB

1.5 cm (⅝ in) turnings allowed on shoulder and side seams

**Each square =
5 cm (2 in)**

Child's Skirt and Bolero (Sizes 2–3, 4–5)   **1** *Make pattern (see p. 41) following diagram above for bolero.*

Child's shirt and bolero.

Child's Skirt and Bolero 2 *Cutting layout. Cut out (see p. 72).* **3** *Bias binding – with folded edges.* **4** *Folded in two, pressed.* **5** *Pressed in a curve to match shape of bolero.*

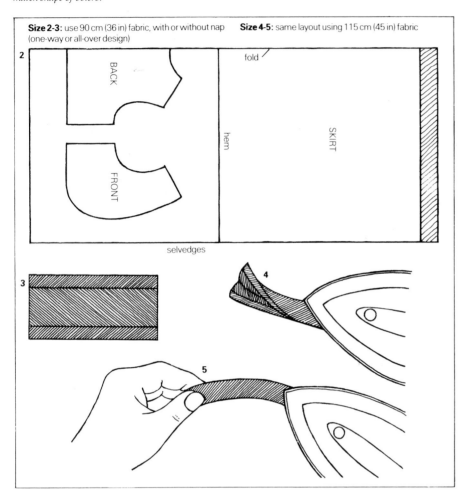

Skirt (cont.)

1 Make a double turn hem (page 34) for the top of the skirt using 2.5 cm (1″). Tack and press.

2 Work at least six rows of shirring (page 32), having the first on the hem edge.

3 With RS together, pin, tack and machine the side seam, and adjust for size if necessary. Machine over the shirred section twice, having the stitching very close together. Press seam open avoiding the elastic.

4 Neaten seam by turning raw edges under 4 mm ($\frac{3}{16}$″), tack, press and zigzag. Stitch seam down by hand over the shirring.

5 Turn up to the required length. Prepare a double turn hem and machine or stitch by hand.

Bolero

1 Make the pattern from the diagram.

2 Cut out in top fabric, wadding and lining.

3 Tack and machine side seam of top fabric and lining. Press seams open.

4 Trim off side and shoulder seam allowance from the wadding. Place this to the WS of top fabric, butting the edges together at the side seams. Lay the lining over the wadding, RS up. Tack the three layers together.

5 Work freehand quilting (page 56), but avoid going too close to the shoulders.

6 Machine stitch shoulder seams, top fabric only, and press open carefully.

7 Hand sew the lining shoulder seam, by turning under on the front piece and smoothing the back towards the front.

8 Zigzag over all raw edges.

9 Fold and press bias binding in two, and curve it into shape, with a medium hot iron, for the armholes and outer edges.

10 Tack into place by inserting the neatened edges to the fold of the bias binding, turning one edge to overlap the other at the join.

11 Zigzag binding into place, with RS up.

12 Press edges only, using a light pressure.

Quickie Skirt

(FROM MEASUREMENTS)

It is better to have success making a simple garment in an easy-to-handle fabric and gradually progress to more difficult styles and materials.

The instructions below are for a skirt with unpressed pleats at centre front and back, and gathers at the sides. There is a bag pocket on the left which is also the opening.

Choose a plain or all-over design of light to medium-weight fabric in a cotton or polyester/cotton. If you use a thicker or stiffer material, the finished skirt will not hang or drape well.

The fabric requirement using 115 cm (45″) width material is worked out by measuring the desired length, adding 9 cm (3⅝″) for hem and waist seam allowance and multiplying by 2.

Calculate the length of the waistband required to be cut as follows: Waist measurement + 2.5 cm (1″) ease + 3 cm (1¼″) seam allowance + 7.5 cm (3″) underlap.

Instructions

1 Make a pattern for the pocket from the diagram. Place single-thickness fabric RS up; make sure that the cut edge is at right angles to the selvedges by checking with a set square or dressmaker's ruler before marking cutting lines – use a metre stick and tailor's chalk, following the diagram.

Machine setting

Presser feet: General/Zigzag
Needle: 80–90
Stitch width: 0 for straight stitch, and 2–2½ for zigzag
Stitch length: 2–2½ for straight stitch and zigzag, and 4 for gathering

Requirements

Fabric: Width 115 cm (45″) – quantity as calculated (purchase 25 cm [10″] extra, if making Easy Top with the facings matching the skirt)
Interfacing: Ultrasoft light iron-on
Firm Fold-a-Band: 7 cm (2¾″) wide
2 hooks and bars
Tacking cotton
Thread
Metric pattern paper

Quickie Skirt *(Sizes 10–18)* **1** *Make pattern for pocket (see p. 41) following top diagram.* **2** *Cutting plan – cut out (see p. 72) from single thickness of*

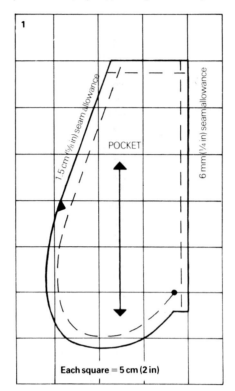

Each square = 5 cm (2 in)

2 The waistband requires to be marked out 8 cm (3¼″) wide; do not use the selvedges.
3 Cut out your skirt, having your scissors to the left of the piece if you are right-handed and to the right if you are left-handed.

fabric RS up, checking that cut edge is at right-angles to the selvedges. Mark dots on LH-side seam 25 cm (10 in) below waist edge. **3** *Stitch pocket*

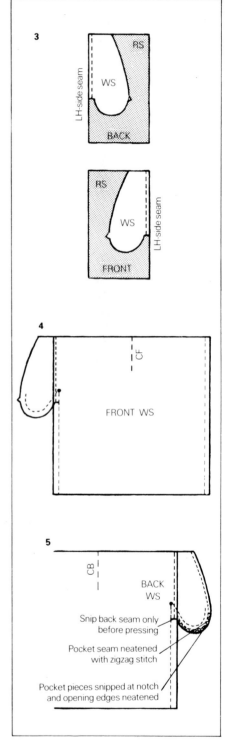

4 Mark the notches and dots as positioned on cutting lay-out. Fold front and back skirt pieces into two, having the side seam edges together to find the centre of each and mark with a tack line.
5 Press Fold-a-Band to the WS of waistband

pieces to front and back skirt on the LH-side seam. **4** Stitch side seams. **5** Pocket pieces, snipped; opening edges neatened; pocket seam neatened; back seam snipped; press. **6** Diagram for pleating and gathering RS uppermost; front and back alike, 'A' goes to 'B'. **7** Marking CF, CB and RH-side seam on RS of waistband. **8** Waistband machined into place; seam trimmed. **9** Hooks and bars sewn in position. **10** Slip-stitching the hem.

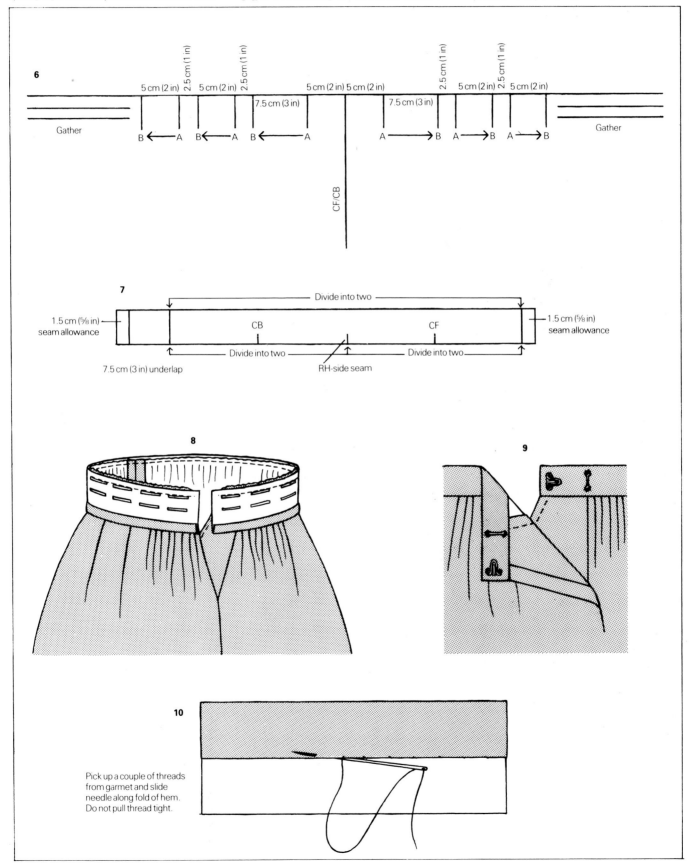

Easy Top
(USING DIAGRAM PATTERN)

Easy top.

An easy top to make from a diagram pattern, if made in the same material as the 'Quickie Skirt' will give the appearance of a dress, when worn together with a belt at the waist. It is a pullover style which is cool and comfortable to wear. There are variations that can be made and the one below uses contrasting fabric to the skirt, with front band opening and facings made from the same material as the skirt. (*Note*: 1.30 m of fabric is still sufficient for making the top, including the facings, in one colour, for all sizes 10–18.)

Machine setting

Presser foot: General/Zigzag
Needle: 80–90
Stitch width: 0 for straight stitch, and $2-2\frac{1}{2}$ for zigzag
Stitch length: $2-2\frac{1}{2}$

Requirements

Fabric: Width 115 cm (45″) – 1.30 m ($1\frac{3}{8}$ yds); contrast for facings – 25 cm (10″)
Interfacing: Ultrasoft light iron-on 40 cm (16″) × 30 cm (12″)
Light Fold-a-Band: 50 cm (20″)
Tacking cotton
Thread
3 buttons: diameter 1.3 cm ($\frac{1}{2}$″)
Metric pattern paper

Instructions

1 Make the pattern from the diagram.
2 Cut out front and back from main fabric, and facings from contrast material (use front band facing pattern from Further Processes **1(c)** on page 43).
3 Transfer markings from pattern to fabric.
4 Cut interfacing for neck facings; trim off seam allowance, and press to WS.
5 Stitch shoulder seams of top front and back, press, neaten, and press again.
6 Join facings at shoulders, trim seams to 6 mm ($\frac{1}{4}$″) and press. Stay-stitch outer edge 6 mm ($\frac{1}{4}$″) from raw edge and, using this as a guide, turn under, tack and press.
7 Place RS of facing to WS of neck edge, tack and machine 1.5 cm ($\frac{5}{8}$″) from raw edges. Trim to 6 mm ($\frac{1}{4}$″), and snip towards stitching.
8 Bring the facing to the RS, rolling seam

(page 45) having the centre slots to the centre of the band; press interfacing to WS of back pocket piece.
6 Stitch pocket pieces to front and back skirt, having RS together, matching notches, taking a 6 mm ($\frac{1}{4}$″) seam; press seam towards pocket.
7 With RS together pin, tack and machine seams, the right-hand side from lower edge to waist, the left-hand side from lower edge to dot; pivot and continue stitching round pocket to the notch; stitch round pocket, again 6 mm ($\frac{1}{4}$″) away from first stitching; trim close to machining; zigzag to neaten.
8 Snip at notch mark and finish opening edges with a narrow hem; reinforce bottom of opening with zigzag. Snip back seam below pocket, and press side seams open; neaten raw edges, and press again.
9 Follow the diagram for pleating, and tack. Keeping pocket pieces free, work two/three rows of gathering (page 45) from the last pleat on each side to side seams and take threads through to back.
10 To find the position on the waistband for the right side seam, place down with RS up and by measurement, mark as shown halfway between the front seam allowance and the back extension and seam allowance; divide these two sections in half to find the positions for centre back and front.
11 Pin waistband to skirt, RS together, matching the points just marked to right side seams, CB, CF, and the extension to the back pocket piece.
12 Pin the pleated section into place working from the centres outwards; pull up bobbin threads and adjust evenly to fit; tack. Fold front pocket section in place, pin and tack.
13 Machine waistband into position, trim seam and press towards the band; then press seam allowance on the other edge of waistband. Fold in two RS together, stitch ends, trim to 6 mm ($\frac{1}{4}$″), and turn RS out. Hem the pressed edge of the band by hand into the machine stitching.
14 Sew hooks and bars on as shown.
15 Turn up hem allowance, tack and press fold. Take out tacking, place raw edge to crease of fold, tack and press before slip-stitching the hem.

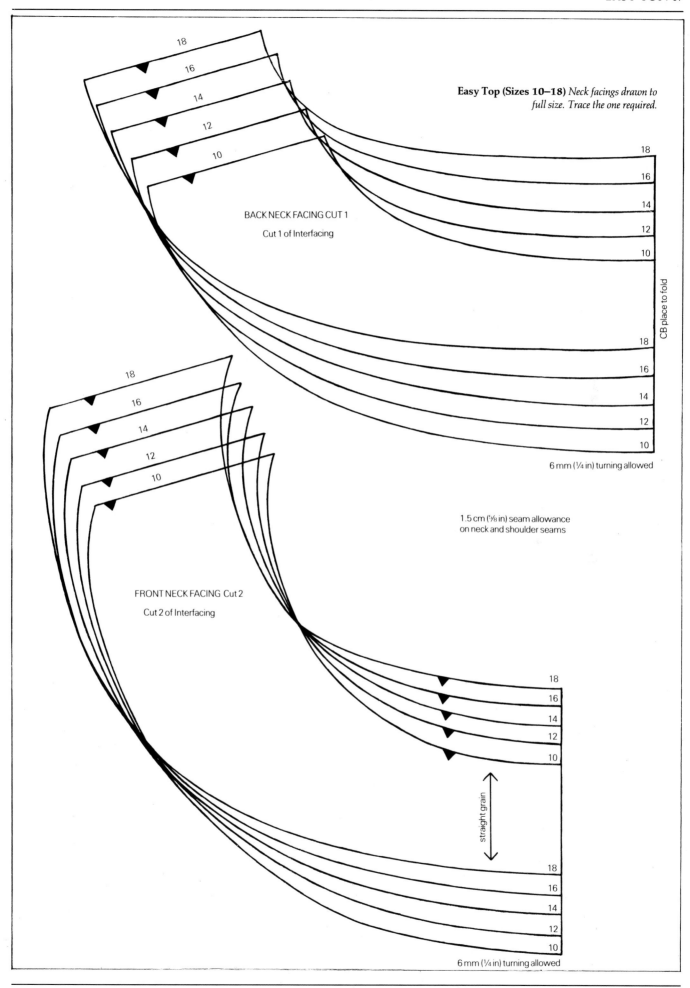

Easy Top (Sizes 10–18) *Neck facings drawn to full size. Trace the one required.*

18
16
14
12
10

BACK NECK FACING CUT 1

Cut 1 of Interfacing

18
16
14
12
10

CB place to fold

18
16
14
12
10

6 mm (¼ in) turning allowed

1.5 cm (⅝ in) seam allowance
on neck and shoulder seams

18
16
14
12
10

FRONT NECK FACING Cut 2

Cut 2 of Interfacing

18
16
14
12
10

straight grain

18
16
14
12
10

6 mm (¼ in) turning allowed

between fingers and thumbs (make sure the seam remains just on the WS). Tack as you go; press edge.

9 Tack the facing into position and edge stitch this and the neck edge.

10 Prepare front band facing with Fold-a-Band; tack and press turnings into position (as in Further Processes **1(c)** on page 44).

11 Matching CF line, place RS of facing to the WS of front, having the top seam allowance above the faced neck edge. Tack and machine into place on the stitching lines, pivoting at the bottom corners. Cut on CF line and diagonally to the corners. Trim seams to 6 mm ($\frac{1}{4}''$).

12 With the RS of the garment up, pull the under band through the cut. Tack the attachment seam towards the band and press. Fold band RS together on the slots, tack and stitch top of band. Trim seam; turn to RS, tack and press. Pin and tack the prepared turning over the machine stitching of the attachment seam to within 2.5 cm (1") of the bottom.

13 Pull top band right through the opening; this will allow the centre bottom seam to be tacked onto the RS and pressed.

14 The tacking of the under band can now be completed, and tacked over the centre bottom seam through all layers.

15 Edge stitch long edges and top of under band. Take out tacking and press.

16 Tack the attachment seam towards the top band and press. Fold band, RS together; tack, stitch and trim top of band as before. After turning the band to the RS, tack pressed edge over the machine stitching, keeping it free of the under band.

17 Edge stitch long edges and top. Pull threads through to the back and knot.

18 Work buttonholes (page 51).

19 Lap top band over the under band, matching centre lines. Tack and edge stitch through all layers, stitching in a square from dot to dot, and pivoting at each corner.

20 Pull threads to back, knot and thread them in. Press.

21 Pin, tack and machine side seams from lower edge to dots at underarm; snip 1.3 cm ($\frac{1}{2}''$) below dots, halfway into seam allowance, before neatening seams.

22 Turn a narrow double hem round armholes and lower edge, and tack. Press both before and after machining; square stitching at underarms.

23 Sew on buttons.

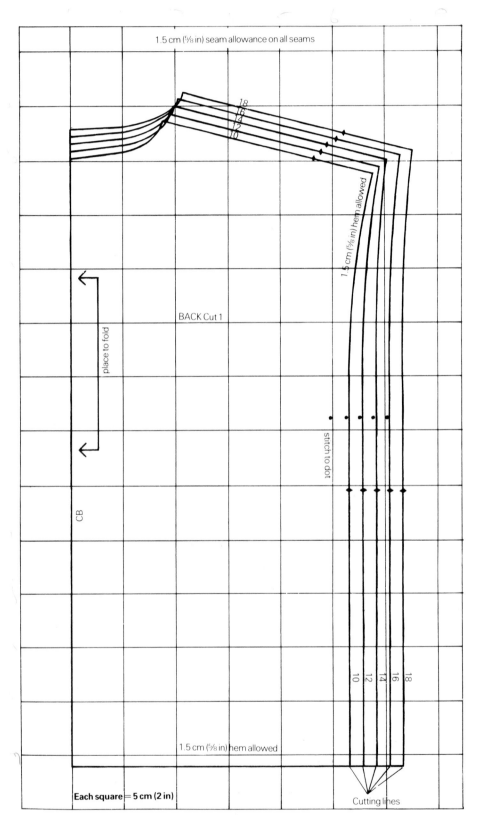

(Above) **Easy Top – Front**   *(Opposite)* **Easy Top – Back**

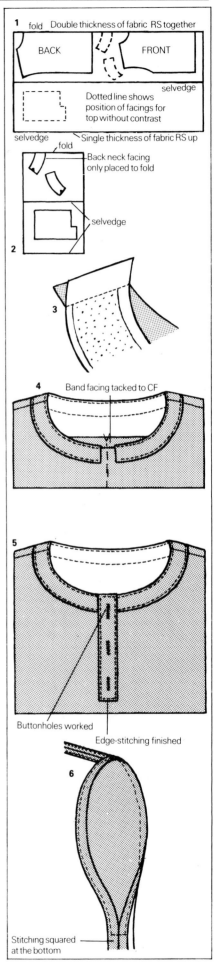

1 fold Double thickness of fabric RS together

BACK   FRONT

selvedge

Dotted line shows position of facings for top without contrast

selvedge   Single thickness of fabric RS up

fold

Back neck facing only placed to fold

selvedge

2

3

4 Band facing tacked to CF

5

Buttonholes worked

Edge-stitching finished

6

Stitching squared at the bottom

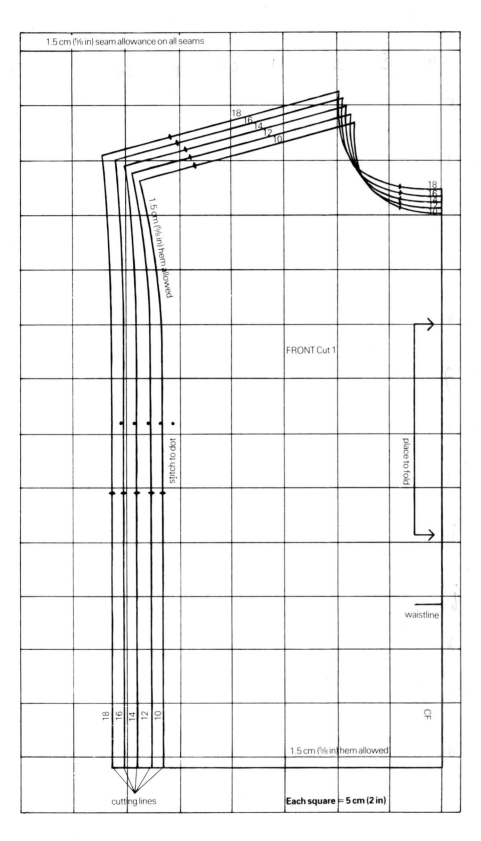

1.5 cm (⅝ in) seam allowance on all seams

18
16
14
12
10

18
16
14
12
10

1.5 cm (⅝ in) hem allowed

FRONT Cut 1

place to fold

stitch to dot

waistline

CF

18 16 14 12 10

1.5 cm (⅝ in) hem allowed

cutting lines

Each square = 5 cm (2 in)

(Right) **Easy Top 1** Cutting layout. **2** Contrast fabric for facings. **3** Facings joined at shoulder seam. **4** Neck facings stitched into place and edge-stitched to the outside. Note: they do not meet in the centre. **5** Band facing complete. **6** Armhole hem.

Patterns

Choosing Patterns

The newcomer to dressmaking is somewhat bewildered at the vast choice available, when starting to buy commercial patterns. 'Where do I begin?' is the question I am constantly asked.

The first step in choosing a pattern is to take the following measurements and write them down: bust/chest, waist, hips, height and length from nape of neck to the waist. To find out which pattern size is nearest to the measurements you have, and to ascertain which would be the correct figure 'type' (Misses, Miss Petite, Womens, etc.), look in the large pattern catalogues available in department stores or fabric shops — in the back are charts for you to compare the measurements you have, with the 'average' ones stated. Read the description against each figure type, as this will guide you to find out which pattern is correct for your build, and so you can decide which type and size would be best to purchase.

Ladies' blouses and dresses are selected by bust measurement, skirts and trousers by waist measurement, unless the hips measure 5 cm (2″) more than the standard difference shown in the charts. In this case purchase by the measurement of the hips, and make an alteration to the waist. It is easier to take in rather than enlarge, especially for the beginner. There is always an exception to every rule and should the skirt be a flared one, purchase the pattern by the waist measurement, as the style will give the extra ease required over the hips.

When buying men's patterns, shirts are selected by the neck size, trousers by waist measurement. Garments for sportswear, pyjamas and bathrobes are generally listed small, medium, and large, with the size range of each stated.

Choose toddlers' and children's, boys' and girls' patterns by their measurements and not by age. Babies' pattern sizes often give weight and height as a guidance, but do remember when sewing for babies and young children that they grow quickly. It is better to make one size too big, they will grow into it, but if it is too small there is very little that one can do.

Most pattern companies have some designs with only a few pattern pieces to contend with — these are referred to as 'Easy', 'Jiffy', 'See and Sew', etc. Look for the garment you want to make in the appropriate section: Blouses and Tops, Skirts and Trousers or whatever, finding the size and figure type that you wish to purchase amongst the 'Easy' ones. You might find some patterns called 'Multisize'; these generally have three sizes in one envelope, but they do have a different cutting line printed on the pattern pieces for each size.

The Pattern Envelope

On the front of the pattern envelope will be an artist's impression of the style(s) and sometimes a photograph too. But it is on the back of the pattern envelope that you will find a wealth of information, which is sometimes confusing for the beginner.

First of all there is a description of the design and the different ways/views it can be made — these are denoted by letters or numbers, e.g. View A or View 1.

There is a body measurement table to check that you have selected the correct size and fabric requirements are listed under each view, with fabric widths quoted on separate lines.

By the fabric widths there is a starred system used by all pattern companies to denote whether the quantity of fabric stated is for a 'With Nap', 'Without Nap', or 'With or Without Nap' cutting layout. 'With Nap' always requires more material as all the pattern pieces have to lay in one direction (definition of the above terms are in 'Choosing Fabrics' on page 60). 'With or Without Nap' means that the pattern pieces are placed in one direction anyway, so that it doesn't make any difference to the amount of fabric required. The starred system is defined on the back of all pattern envelopes, although different companies do have slight variations.

Also stated on the envelope is the length of a garment and width at the hemline. Suggested fabrics for the design are given, and this is a good guideline for the beginner, especially as to what would be suitable for the style.

Notions, too, are specified. This tells you what haberdashery to purchase, the length of a zip (if one is required), the size of buttons, thread, hooks and bars, shoulder pads, and so on. Interfacing is sometimes in this section or on a separate line.

Instruction Sheet and Pattern

The instruction sheet inside the pattern envelope is the next source of information. The 'Cutting Layouts' are diagrams showing the positioning of the pattern pieces on the fabric, ready for cutting out. The layouts are in sections for each view and alongside each diagram it states the fabric width, which sizes it is relating to and whether it is for a 'With' or 'Without Nap' fabric, or one that can be used for either because the pattern pieces are placed in one direction, because of the width of the fabric.

Find the appropriate diagram in your size, chosen fabric (width and type), and the view you wish to make, and draw a ring around it. This will attract your eye every time you want to refer to it, and also eliminate the chance of following the wrong one. A feature of cutting layouts is the shading of some pattern pieces; this shading denotes that the printed side of the pattern requires to be placed face down onto the fabric.

Immediately by the view identification, the pattern pieces required will be listed. These will want the surplus tissue trimmed off, and it is better to do this exactly on the cutting line; this gives a more precise cut to the fabric and your pattern remains in perfect condition for future use, and patterns are often used more than once.

There are some patterns that do not give a seam allowance. They are printed on thin paper instead of on tissue paper and are all multi-size; these require to be trimmed on the size line. When using these patterns, the seam allowances and hem have to be marked on the fabric after the pattern pieces have been pinned into position. Leave sufficient space in between each one for this to be done, either by a special seam allowance tracing wheel, which has powdered chalk in a small bottle over the wheel, thus leaving a line to follow when cutting out, or by a small slide rule/tape measure and tailor's chalk. This must be carried out precisely following the pattern company's instructions.

Pattern Marks and Symbols

Last, but by no means least, there are further instructions and information printed on the actual pattern pieces. There are various marks and symbols which are all important and need to be observed. Some relate to the cutting out stage, and some to the construction of the garment. The pattern companies vary a little, but they all give a definition of symbols, etc. on the instruction sheet.

Straight grain/Lengthwise grain is the first instruction to note as you are placing the pattern pieces to your fabric. The straight line, with or without arrowheads, has to be parallel with the selvedge; it is essential to measure this and not place it just by eye. Accurate placement of this line gives the garment the correct hang. If it isn't placed on the straight grain of the fabric, the garment will be inclined to twist round in wear – and this point applies to sleeves especially.

Place to fold is a straight line with the ends turned at right angles, with arrowheads pointing towards the fold when in position on the fabric. Any pattern pieces with 'Place to Fold' printed on are cut from double thickness of material with the fold made on the 'straight grain'; the fold becomes the centre of the garment piece.

Cutting line is either a thick line or scissor symbol (or your own chalk line, if you are working with a pattern without a seam allowance).

Notches are balance marks along the cutting lines. If you cut these outwards, as you are cutting out your garment, it saves time not having to mark them on your fabric by some other means, before removing the pattern. These notches are numbered, and during construction will be matched to another notch having the same number. These numbers are also a guide to the order of making a garment.

Stitching/Seam line is normally 1.5 cm ($\frac{5}{8}''$) from the cutting line; it is marked on most printed tissue patterns, either by a broken line, or by a presser foot symbol. The exceptions are the Multisize tissue patterns that do have the seam allowance included, although this isn't shown by a printed line, and the thin paper patterns which require the seam allowance to be marked on the fabric after pinning the pattern into place. All patterns clearly state instructions about the seam allowance and stitching line, and whether these differ from the normal 1.5 cm ($\frac{5}{8}''$).

Cutting Out and Marking

Press fabric (pages 20, 60). Draw a ring around the chosen cutting layout diagram. Fold material – RS together if double fabric is required, and RS uppermost when pattern pieces are going to be cut from a single thickness of material.

Place on a flat surface (a cardboard cutting board on a dining table is ideal), since the fabric should not be on anything it will cling to, as this would make it very difficult to get the material laying flat. Aligning the selvedges together when the material is required double, ensures that the fabric is on the straight grain; the raw cut edges may not be straight, so do not attempt to try and have these aligned as well. It is the lengthwise grain running parallel to the selvedges that is so very important. Do not allow your fabric to hang over the end of the table, for this can have a tendency to pull it off the straight, so support it on a chair.

If you wish to allow extra on the seams of a garment, always mark with tailor's chalk a precise measurement using a slide-rule, never just guess. 1 cm ($\frac{3}{8}''$) is an ideal *extra* allowance – this would then make a 2.5 cm (1″) seam. This is only necessary if you have to enlarge a garment a little, e.g. the side seams of a skirt, owing to the pattern measurements being less than those required. If necessary lengthen or shorten pattern pieces, using the lines indicated on the pattern, before placing them on your fabric. This again requires to be done with precision.

Position pattern pieces following the layout. Anchor each one in the first instance with scissors or a pin box, etc., just to keep it from moving until you have made sure the straight grain lines on the pattern pieces are parallel to the selvedges, by measuring them.

After checking, place a couple of pins along the straight grain line, before continuing to pin the pattern to the fabric. Do not use too many pins, and do not place them near the edge of the pattern, except when using a fabric that 'pin marks' – then the pins have to be placed within the seam allowance, or masking tape has to be used on a paper pattern that does not have any seam allowance. Pin all pattern pieces into place before cutting out.

Cut out, having your scissors to the left of the pattern if you are right-handed, and to the right if you are left-handed. Cut precisely on the cutting line, cutting outwards to denote the balance marks/notches as you come to them. Read any cutting out instructions on the pattern pieces to ensure that you have understood what is required, e.g. place to fold, cut 2, etc.

Transfer all markings, e.g. for darts, required in the construction of the garment from the pattern to the fabric, except any piece that needs interfacing. This should be pressed into position first and the marking done afterwards. If you marked with tailor's tacks, then pressed interfacing on the fabric, this would literally bond the tacks in and they would be difficult to remove, without tugging at them, and this could disturb the interfacing causing marks on the material.

There are several different methods of transferring pattern markings to fabric. They are described below giving a guide line when each should be used. Generally, more than one method is used on a garment.

Tailor's Tacks: a double looped stitch which can be used on any material worked with an appropriate sized needle, threaded with tacking cotton, and using a long double thread without a knot.

It can be worked through the pattern and two layers of fabric as follows: take a small stitch through all layers, leave an end; make another stitch in the same place, leave a loop; again another stitch to leave a second loop, cut off threads leaving an end. This method is suitable for dots, or any pattern symbol that indicates matching with a like symbol, e.g. dots for a dart, dots for placement of sleeve in an armhole, gathering a longer edge to fit into a shorter one. To remove pattern from the fabric, cut the top loops and lift tissue away; gently part the two layers of material and snip the threads in between.

Tailor's Tacking: is looped tacking, and is worked in a similar way to the above method, but in a continuous line just leaving one loop on each stitch. It is ideal for seam lines, placement of pockets, anywhere a line is to be marked, on two layers of fabric.

Turn back pattern to the line you wish to mark, folding exactly on the line. Work with a double thread, no knot, and tacking as near as possible to the pattern, take a stitch 6 mm ($\frac{1}{4}''$); leave 2 cm ($\frac{3}{4}''$) before the next stitch of 6 mm ($\frac{1}{4}''$); continue in this manner. After completing the tacking, snip all top stitches. Pull the two layers of material gently apart and snip the threads in between.

Tailor's Chalk: is available in different forms and in various colours. In powder for use with a special tracing wheel, it is placed in a small plastic bottle, which is fixed over a small wheel that can be adjusted to give varying widths away from the main wheel. This can be run by the side of patterns which do not include a seam allowance – the chalk leaves a line on the fabric quickly marking a cutting line.

Tailor's chalk is available in a firm substance, in a triangle or square shape and can be used on the WS of fabric for quick marking. It is inadvisable to use on the RS, as pressing can make it semi-permanent on some fabrics. There is also a chalk pencil that is very useful.

Dressmaking Carbon Paper and Tracing Wheel: cut the carbon paper into strips as this makes it easier to manipulate. Place the strips, carbon side to the WS of the fabric, and using a smooth tracing wheel and a small steel ruler, mark darts, small lines, etc.

Ideal on thick cotton or wool fabrics, it does have a tendency to be permanent when pressing is done. Do not use on thin materials, and always test on medium weight fabrics by marking and pressing, to check whether it penetrates through to the RS.

Fabric Pens: several are available, some are removed by water or washing, some fade away, but all require testing on the fabric you are working with to make sure they are removable or do fade. If all is well after testing, they have the advantage of being able to be used on the RS of the fabric.

Pins: last but by no means least. The small-headed type can be pushed through the pattern to the double layer of fabric, the pattern removed, and a chalk line drawn, first on one side then on the other to mark darts, etc. In fact, any symbol can be marked first with a pin and then by chalk or tacking. If it is a 'Quickie' garment, the pin marking method can be used without any additional marking.

Classic Skirt

(PURCHASED PATTERN)

A gently flared A-line skirt is easy to make and comfortable to wear. Choose a plain fabric of medium weight – a linen type weave or a wool blend is ideal; either will handle and press well. All the processes used have been practised except one, which is stitching darts, so you can feel confident in making a garment with a good end result.

Machine setting

Presser feet: General/Zigzag and Zipper
Needle: 80–90
Stitch width: 0 for straight stitch, and $2\frac{1}{2}$–3 for zigzag
Stitch length: 2–$2\frac{1}{2}$ for straight and zigzag stitching, and 4 for easing stitch

Requirements

Pattern
Fabric and zip: As stated on pattern envelope
Interfacing: Fold-a-Band
Tacking cotton
Thread
Hooks and bars

Instructions

1 Draw a ring around the appropriate cutting lay-out, trim pattern and iron with a warm dry iron.
2 Press fabric with a damp muslin and medium/hot iron, pressing out the fold line if there is one.
3 If you have selected the correct pattern from your measurements, the skirt should not require much alteration. If your waist is smaller than the pattern, take in a little on all the seams, remembering that the waistband will require shortening, otherwise there will be too much underlap. If you have to enlarge the waist, extra seam allowance should be allowed during the cutting out stage (page 72) and the waistband too should be lengthened.
4 Fold the material, as indicated in layout diagram, place pattern on fabric, remembering to measure the straight grain arrows to the selvedge making sure they are parallel, and pin in place using only a few pins.
5 Cut out, having the scissors to the left of the pattern if you are right-handed and to

Classic Skirt *(purchased pattern)* **1** *Sample layout.*　　**2** *Sewing darts.* **3** *Trimming waist seam.*

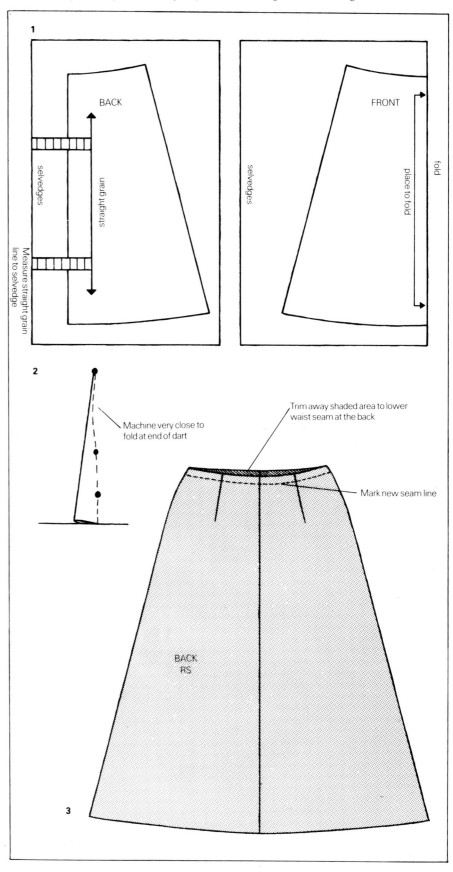

the right if you are left-handed.

6 Transfer markings from pattern to fabric (page 72).

7 Stay-stitch waist edge.

8 It is advisable to tack the darts and seams, and try on the skirt before machining, so follow through the preparation stages in the instructions, bypassing the machining. If possible enlist the help of a friend for pinning the adjustments when fitting. Tack any alterations and try on again before proceeding with the machining.

9 Pin and tack the darts, matching dots, from the waist edge downwards, machine in the same direction. The secret of a good dart is to avoid finishing sewing abruptly. Taper down towards the end and sew very near the fold for a few stitches (see diagram) leaving thread ends long enough to knot before cutting them shorter. (Note: This is a more satisfactory method of finishing a dart, for reverse stitching can cause a pucker at the end of a dart on some fabrics; also should you need to unpick the machine stitching for any reason, it would be difficult to avoid making a hole in the material.) There are generally darts on the front and back of a classic skirt, and they are longer on the back than the front. Do make sure that each pair of darts is exactly the same length, measure before machining and mark the finishing points with a pin.

10 Press darts in the same direction as stitching, wide to narrow and towards the centre front and centre back, preferably over a curved pressing pad; darts give shaping which would only be pressed out if you used a flat surface.

11 Pin, tack and machine seams, press; neaten and press again.

12 Prepare left-hand side opening and insert zip (page 53).

13 Press Fold-a-Band to waistband, pin and tack to waist, RS together, matching all markings; if you have a sway/hollow back, lower the waistband at the back (see diagram); also remember if you have taken in or enlarged, then allow for the adjustments.

14 Machine to skirt using slots as your guide. Trim seam to 1 cm ($\frac{3}{8}''$); press turnings towards band.

15 Tack and press the seam allowance, using the slots as your guide, on the other edge of the waistband trimming the seam allowance to 6 mm ($\frac{1}{4}''$).

16 Fold on centre slots, RS together, stitch

ends, trim to 6 mm ($\frac{1}{4}''$); turn to RS and making sure the seam is on the edge, press.

17 Pin the prepared edge of waistband over the machine stitching, placing the pins at the right side seam, CF, CB, and at the opening LH side. (Note: The waistband will extend 2.5 cm [1″] – 4 cm [1$\frac{1}{2}$″] beyond the LH side of the skirt at the back.)

18 Turn up hem to the desired length; tack near to the bottom and press the fold. Measure the depth of the hem from the fold, 4 cm (1$\frac{1}{2}$″); mark with tailor's chalk and trim to this line.

19 Zigzag raw edge, machine 6 mm ($\frac{1}{4}''$) from neatened edge using stitch length 4; pull up the bobbin thread a little to ease the fullness, so that the hem will lie flat against the skirt.

20 Tack just below the machine stitching. Catch stitch by hand, having the fold towards you, and holding the neatened edge down on the eased machine stitch line, so that the stitching takes place 6 mm ($\frac{1}{4}''$) under the hem edge. Having the stitching below the edge makes the hem literally invisible. (Catch stitch, page 33.) Give a final press.

Classic skirt and shirt. See pages 73, 76.

Classic Shirt

(PURCHASED PATTERN)

This is a style that is always 'right' for everyday wear. It looks smart and can be made in a variety of fabrics – woven cotton, brushed cotton, cotton blended with polyester or wool (having at least 50% cotton fibres).

Classic shirt patterns generally have a choice of collars and cuffs, and usually can be made with or without a yoke or a pocket. From the description on the back of the pattern envelope, you will be able to make your choice of which view to make.

There is only one process in making this garment that hasn't been practised and that is putting in sleeves. With a traditional shirt style they are attached flat, to enable top stitching to be done before the sleeve and side seams.

Machine setting

Presser feet: General and Buttonhole
Needle: 80–90
Stitch width: 0 for straight stitch, and buttonhole setting
Stitch length: 2–2½ for straight stitch, and nearly 0 for buttonholes

Requirements

Pattern
Fabric: As stated on pattern envelope
Buttons
Interfacing: Ultrasoft light iron-on
Wundaweb
Tacking cotton
Thread

Instructions

1 Draw a ring around your chosen 'view' cutting lay-out.
2 Read through the instruction sheet, finding the steps/stages that are appropriate for your view and mark the ones you will be following with a coloured felt tip pen or pencil. (Note: This will save time whilst making the garment, especially if there are several collars that can be used with the same body pieces. Sleeves too sometimes have a choice of cuffs or methods of neatening the opening, so marking the ones you have decided to use before you begin will make for quicker progress when you are sewing.)

It is wise to learn how to follow the instruction sheets that accompany patterns – after all, they have been tried and tested before being included in the pattern catalogues. Here is a guideline to the order of work with reminders of the Practice Plans that you have already done. Remember that pressing is required after each stage and also as stated.

1 Trim pattern pieces required; iron with warm dry iron.
2 Press fabric, using a damp muslin if necessary.
3 Fold fabric as cutting lay-out.
4 Place and pin pattern into position, remembering to measure that the straight grain arrows are parallel with the selvedge.
5 Cut out all pieces.
6 Transfer markings from pattern to fabric, except where interfacing is required, and only remove the pattern when the piece is required for a further process.
7 Cut out interfacing, probably using the same pattern piece that you have used for the collar band, under collar and cuffs; this will be printed on the pattern, but there is generally a separate pattern piece for the front strip.
8 Press interfacing into position after trimming away the seam allowance.
9 Replace patterns and transfer markings, except buttonholes.
10 Prepare fronts by pressing the fold line and seam allowance ready to neaten the facings by stitching down. Before machining the right front, place a small strip of Wundaweb directly where each buttonhole is going to be worked, marking each just with a pin, which should be removed before pressing. Stitch facings down, and mark buttonholes by the tacking method, these will be on the CF line (see diagram).
11 Stitch pocket into position, if there is one on your 'view' (page 29).
12 Machine yoke in place or shoulder seams.
13 Edge stitch yoke or neaten seams.
14 Make up shirt collar (page 49).
15 Attach collar, but before edge stitching the collar band down, insert Wundaweb where the buttonhole is required.
16 Neaten sleeve opening.
17 Attach sleeves by placing RS together with armhole edge, matching circles, dots and notches. With the raw edges even, pin

the sleeve to the garment at these points placing the pins from the raw edges inwards; ease any slight fullness by pinning in the same manner, dividing each section in two, again and again, until it is completely pinned. Tack, using small stitches, removing pins as you work along the seam. Machine into place sleeve uppermost. Press seam away from the sleeve, snipping a little as required to enable it to lie flat; tack, edge stitch and trim. Alternatively use Basic Processes **2(b)** or **(c)** (pages 26–27). (Note: If using **2(b)**, it is the WS together for the first machine stitching.)
18 Machine side and sleeve seams, using the method already adopted when attaching the sleeve; take care to press the seams towards the back.
19 Attach cuffs to sleeves (pp. 44–45). For a true shirt style, instead of gathers there are generally pleats, which of course your pattern will have shown, but the cuff is machined into place in the same manner whether there are gathers or pleats at the bottom of sleeves.
20 Work narrow hem round bottom of shirt (page 34).
21 Work machine buttonholes (page 51).
22 Sew buttons in place.
23 Final press.

If the pattern chosen is more of a blouse type garment with set-in sleeves, the side seams and sleeve seams are machined and neatened, and the cuffs attached, before the sleeves are put in. The procedure would then be as follows:

1 With the sleeve RS out, and the garment WS out push the sleeve into the armhole and working from the inside of the sleeve, align the side and sleeve seams and pin.
2 Match the balance marks, generally a single notch at the front and a double notch at the back, and pin these and all the underarm section, placing the pins in the normal way along the seam line.
3 Match the dots on the sleeve head, with dots and the shoulder seam on the armhole, and placing the pins from the raw edges inwards, continue in a similar manner to the shirt sleeve, dividing each section in two, again and again, until all the fullness has been evenly distributed. (Note: This is easier to accomplish if the sleeve head is arranged over the hand by pushing the shoulder seam into the sleeve.)

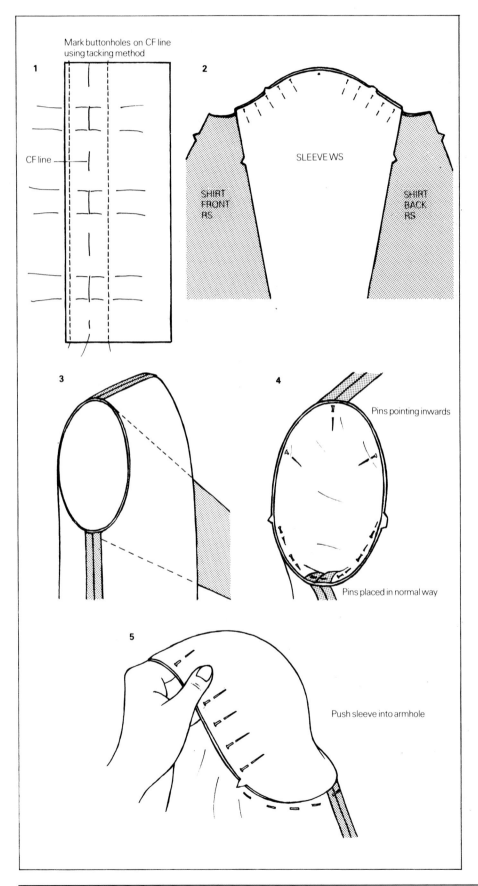

1 Mark buttonholes on CF line using tacking method

CF line

2 SLEEVE WS

SHIRT FRONT RS

SHIRT BACK RS

4 Pins pointing inwards

Pins placed in normal way

5 Push sleeve into armhole

4 Tack with small stitches on the seam line, only removing the pins as you are passing them.

5 Machine the sleeves in, working within the armhole keeping carefully to the seam line; machine a second line of stitching 6 mm ($\frac{1}{4}$") nearer the raw edge. Trim close to stitching.

6 Press the seams towards the sleeves except for the underarm section which does not require any pressing.

7 When making a blouse with a gathered head, work two rows of gathering between the dots as indicated on the pattern. Place one row just within the seam allowance and the other one 6 mm ($\frac{1}{4}$") nearer the raw edge. (Note: Some patterns state that a gathering thread should be inserted for an 'eased' head. In fact, this is generally not required.)

Classic Shirt (*purchased pattern*) **1** *Mark buttonholes on CF line, using tacking method.* **2** *Attach shirt-style sleeves flat, before side and sleeve seams worked.* **3** *Set-in sleeves showing sleeve pushed into armholes.* **4** *Pinning sleeve to armhole of garment, RS together. Match dots on sleeve head, placing pins pointing inwards. Underarm seam with pins placed in normal way on the seam line from single notch to double notches.* **5** *Shoulder seam pushed into sleeve head.*

PART FIVE

Items for Gifts and the Home

Ribbon and lace trimmed bed cushions. See page 96.

(**Opposite**) *Kitchen curtains in cotton ginham.*
(**Below**) *Towelling bathroom curtain showing heading-tape and hooks. See page 80.*

Kitchen

Cotton gingham is an easy care fabric for kitchen curtains. It always seems a cheerful material that comes up smiling even after repeated washing and ironing, and it also takes kindly to machine sewing. Make a plan of the window and curtain track position, to calculate the fabric required. In the example shown, the curtains were made to hang within the window recess.

Calculating length of curtain

	cm	inches
Track to window sill	91	36
Minus clearance of sill	1.5	$\frac{5}{8}$
	89.5	$35\frac{3}{8}$
Extra for heading	4.5	$1\frac{3}{4}$
Extra for hem	9	$3\frac{1}{2}$
Length of fabric required for each curtain	103	$40\frac{5}{8}$

Calculating width of curtain

	cm	inches
Length of track	102	40
Extra for curtain fullness	51	20
	153	60

One width of 90 cm (36″) is necessary for each curtain.

Gingham is made in 90 cm (36″) width so fabric required is: $103 \times 2 = 206$ cm

Machine setting

Presser foot: General
Needle: 90
Stitch width: 0
Stitch length: 2–2½

Requirements

Fabric: Gingham width 90 cm (36″)
– 2.10 m (2⅜ yds)
Rufflette Standard Tape: 1.80 m
(2 yds)
Tacking cotton
Thread

(**Note:** Turn hems etc., using the
squares, as near as possible to
measurements. Press well at each
stage.)

$(40\frac{5}{8}'' \times 2 = 81\frac{1}{4}'')$. The amount of fabric to
be purchased is 2.10 m (2⅜ yds) which gives
a margin for straightening the cut edge.

Instructions

1 Straighten one cut edge, being guided by
the squares, trim off selvedges.
2 Measure length for curtains and cut,
taking care that the two curtains start and
finish on the same colour square.
3 Make a double hem on both sides of each
curtain (page 34) using the allowance of
3 cm $(1\frac{1}{4}'')$.
4 Turn 4.5 cm $(1\frac{3}{4}'')$ at the top of each
curtain, pin and tack.
5 Neaten one end of heading tape, having
pulled the cords to the RS.
6 Position tape 3 cm $(1\frac{1}{4}'')$ from fold at top
of curtain, pin and tack. (Check that the top
fold will clear the ceiling of the window

recess when in position.)
7 Machine tape in place, working in same
direction.
8 Turn a double hem at bottom of curtains,
using the hem allowance of 9 cm $(3\frac{1}{2}'')$.
9 Machine hem.
10 Knot heading cords at one end; pull up
the cords at the other end to gather, so each
curtain measures 53.5 cm (21″).
11 Position hooks in tape, approx every
8 cm (3″). Hang curtains on track runners.

Kitchen Curtains *Plan of window and position of
curtain track.*

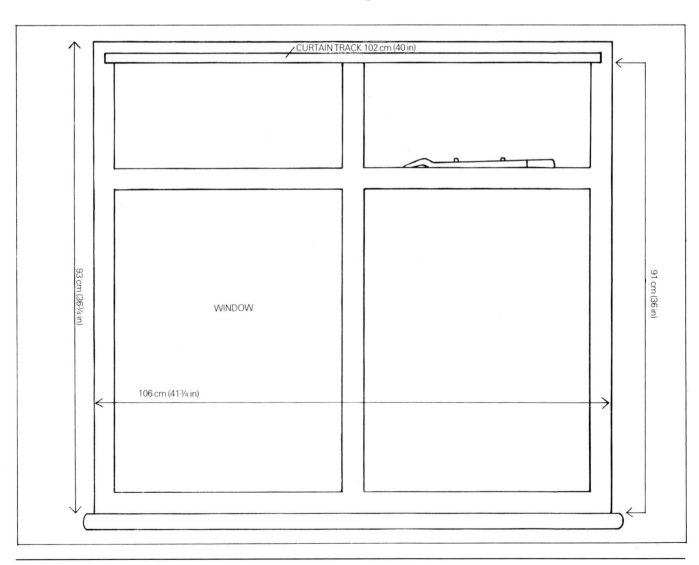

2 Table Linen

(Below) **Table Linen 1** *Table showing measurements.* **2** *Cutting plan.* **3–8** *Making mitred corner, double-turn hem.*

Making tableclothes, serviettes, placemats, trolley and tray clothes is very pleasing. One can choose the fabric to match or contrast with decor, whether it is for everyday use or for a special occasion. Polyester/cotton sheeting, which is available in many designs, will withstand repeated laundering – it is an economical purchase as the width is 228 cm (90″). Cotton and cotton mixtures can also be used. The width of the fabric needs to be known before making a plan to calculate the amount to purchase.

Machine setting

Presser foot: General/Zigzag
Needle: 90
Stitch width: 0 for straight stitch, and $1–1\frac{1}{2}$ for zigzag
Stitch length: $2–2\frac{1}{2}$ for straight stitch, and $\frac{1}{2}–1$ for zigzag

Requirements

Fabric: Sheeting width 228 cm (90″) – 2 metres ($2\frac{1}{4}$ yds)
Crochet cotton for trim
Tacking cotton
Thread

Tablecloth and Serviettes

When making a tablecloth for a particular table, the overhang can be made to be uniform all round, which gives a much better appearance than having a little at the sides but a lot at each end. The example given shows how to determine the material required. It is very necessary to make a cutting-out plan before purchasing the fabric.

Table Measurement	cm	inches
Table length	140	55
Table width	90	$35\frac{1}{2}$

An overhang of 20 cm (8″) and a hem allowance of 8 cm (3″) is required.

Calculate fabric for tablecloth using the measurements.

	cm	inches
Table length	140	55
Overhang	40	16
Hem allow. × 2	16	6
	196	77
Table width	90	$35\frac{1}{2}$
Overhang × 2	40	16
Hem allow. × 2	16	6
	146	$57\frac{1}{2}$

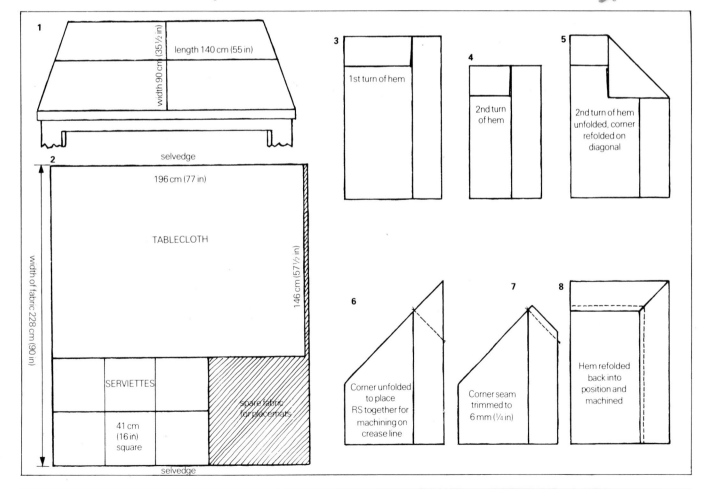

1 width 90 cm (35½ in) · length 140 cm (55 in)

2 selvedge · 196 cm (77 in) · width of fabric 228 cm (90 in) · 146 cm (57½ in) · TABLECLOTH · SERVIETTES · 41 cm (16 in) square · Spare fabric for placemats · selvedge

3 1st turn of hem

4 2nd turn of hem

5 2nd turn of hem unfolded, corner refolded on diagonal

6 Corner unfolded to place RS together for machining on crease line

7 Corner seam trimmed to 6 mm (¼ in)

8 Hem refolded back into position and machined

Tablecloth, placemat and serviette.

The tablecloth length requires to be cut on the straight grain and for the example measurements quoted, 2 metres of 228 cm (90″) width fabric is needed. The cutting out plan shows how this is used to the best advantage.

The serviettes are cut 41 cm (16″) square, with a hem allowance of 4 cm (1½″) (Note: Serviettes can be from 30 cm [12″] to 50 cm [20″]).

The spare fabric can be used to make a small cloth for a side table, or two placemats.

Instructions

1 Make sure the cut edge is at right angles to the selvedge (page 81).
2 Trim off selvedges.
3 Carefully measure the required size for your tablecloth, using a metre stick and pencil.
4 Measure and mark out for six serviettes.
5 Cut out tablecloth and serviettes.
6 Turn 4 cm (1½″) on all edges of tablecloth; press fold. Turn 4 cm (1½″) again, to form a double hem and press.

7 Form mitred corners; unfold the second turn of hem, refold corner on diagonal, press. Unfold. With RS together, machine on crease; trim to 6 mm (¼″). Press seam open and refold hem back into position. (See diagrams.)
8 Tack hem and machine.
9 To give an extra finishing touch, zigzag a crochet cotton over the machine stitch on the RS; butt the cord edges to join.
10 Make serviettes using the same method with a 4 cm (1½″) hem allowance.

Placemats

An average size placemat is 45 cm (18″) × 30 cm (12″), but they can be made to suit individual needs. Follow the hem instructions with mitred corners and use a trim of your choice, from the decorative processes in this book: or quilt the placemats, round the corners and bind the edges.

Appliqué Cushion Cover *(below)* **1** *Cutting plan.* **2** *Round corners of front piece, cut away shaded areas.* **3** *Join bias strips.* **4** *Seam of bias strip pressed open.* **5** *Piping cord enclosed in bias strip,* which *should be stretched slightly as it is being machined.* **6** *To finish off piping — cut piping straight across, cut cord to meet the other end, turn under bias casing.*

Quilted Cushion Cover *(bottom)* **1** *Cutting plan.* **2** *Tack three layers (mull muslin, wadding and fabric) together ready for quilting.* **3** *Pin ruffle to cushion front.*

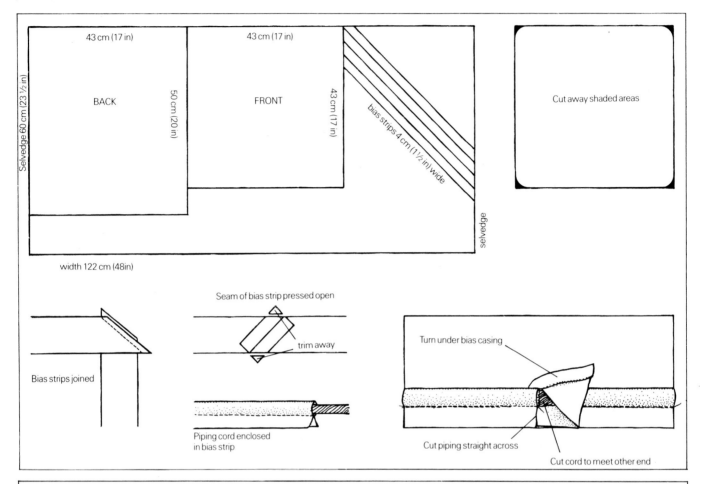

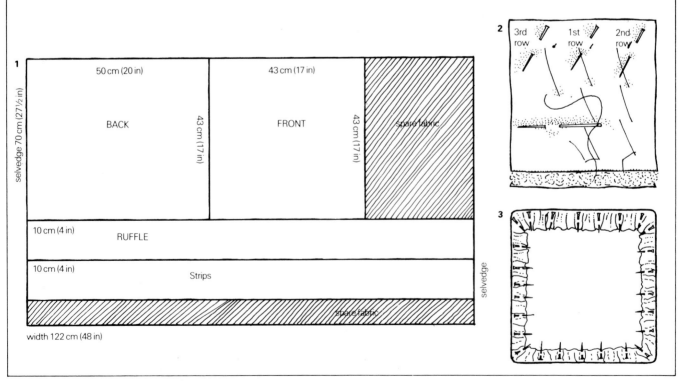

3 Cushion Covers

Cushions, in one form or another, have been in use for a long time, and indeed are very much in evidence today. They can bring colour to a room setting or make a chair or settee more invitingly comfortable. Their use is endless and so is the choice of fabrics.

Cushion covers can be made literally from any type of material, but it has to be chosen with the function it is going to fulfil in mind. Well-made covers in a good quality furnishing fabric will both look good, and withstand a fair amount of wear and tear. The instructions for the four cushion covers that follow fall into this category.

Cushion pads can be purchased ready-made, but are quite easy to make. Thin cotton can be used when the filling is polyester, but feather-proof ticking must be used for feathers; these do 'plump up' nicely and retain their 'new' look, although, poly-ester filled pads have the advantage of being completely washable. The size of a cushion pad needs to be 1.3 cm ($\frac{1}{2}$") larger all round than the cushion cover – this makes for a smooth fit, right to the corners.

(**Note:** If making more than one cushion cover using the same fabric, or having them a different size, calculate the fabric requirements, as a more economical lay-out could be possible.)

Appliqué

The appliqué was chosen from a piece of furnishing fabric left over from making curtains – it is an excellent way of linking a room.

Instructions

1 Cut fabric as in diagram.
2 Cut out motifs from contrasting fabric, leaving a margin all round.
3 Press Bondaweb to the WS of the motifs.
4 Allow to cool. Cut out shapes; peel off backing paper.
5 Position them on front piece of cushion cover; press into place.
6 Zigzag round the motifs, having placed Stitch'n'Tear (or thin typing paper) at the back first.
7 Tear away backing. Place RS down onto a thick pad, and press on WS.
8 Slightly round corners of front piece (see diagram).

Machine setting

Presser feet: General/Zigzag and Zipper
Needle: 90
Stitch width: 0 for straight stitch, $1\frac{1}{2}$–2 for zigzag appliqué, and 2–$2\frac{1}{2}$ for zigzag neatening
Stitch length: 2–$2\frac{1}{2}$ for straight stitch, $\frac{1}{2}$–1 for zigzag appliqué, and 2–$2\frac{1}{2}$ for zigzag neatening

Requirements

Fabric: Width 122 cm (48") – 60 cm ($23\frac{1}{2}$")
Furnishing fabric motifs for appliqué
Tacking cotton
Thread: Matching fabric and appliqué
Piping Cord No. 3: 1.65 m (65")
Velcro: 30 cm (12")
Bondaweb
Stitch'n'Tear
Cushion pad

(**Note:** Wash piping to pre-shrink.)

9 Join bias strips and press seams open.
10 Place piping cord to the WS of the strip, in the centre; fold strip over to enclose the cord. Pin and tack, with raw edges even.
11 Machine as close as possible to the cord, with the zipper foot in position.
12 Pin and tack the piping into position to the RS of front piece, raw edges even, starting in the centre of the bottom edge. Snip seam allowance of piping round corners. Leave an overlap of piping of 2.5 cm (1"), but do not tack.
13 Starting 2.5 cm (1") from end of piping, machine into place, stopping 2.5 cm (1") from the other end.
14 Cut piping straight across on the first end. Turn back bias strip to cut cord only at the other end, making sure the cord will butt together. Turn under the bias casing to neaten, and allow this to cover the raw edge of the first end; complete machining piping into place.
15 Fold back of cushion cover in half and cut to make two pieces 43 cm (17") × 25 cm (10").
16 Turn 2.5 cm (1") to the WS of the centre cut edges. Pin and tack; machine raw edge

down with zigzag stitch, having the correct presser foot in position.
17 Place the back onto a flat surface RS up with an overlap of 2.5 cm (1") in the centre.
18 Stitch 30 cm (12") length of the soft section of Velcro to the top piece of the back on the WS, over the neatened hem, using zigzag stitch.
19 Stitch the hard section to the RS of the lower piece of the back, aligning the Velcro to make a neat closure. Fasten the Velcro.
20 Place the front and back, RS together, pin, tack and machine using the stitch line from attaching the piping to the front, as a guide, and having the zipper foot in position.
21 Trim seam to 1 cm ($\frac{3}{8}$"); zigzag to neaten (using zigzag presser foot).
22 Snip into corners a little, turn to RS. Press if required, avoiding the piping.

Quilted

The design for a quilted cushion cover can be obtained from various sources, traced from wallpaper, magazines, or books, it can be drawn 'freehand', or a transfer could be used. Whatever is chosen needs to be simple, with easy-to-negotiate curves and angles for machine quilting.

Machine setting

Presser feet: General and Quilting or Embroidery
Needle: 90
Stitch width: 0 for straight stitch and quilting, and $1\frac{1}{2}$–2 for satin stitch
Stitch length: 2–$2\frac{1}{2}$ for straight stitch, $\frac{1}{2}$–1 for satin stitch, and 4 for quilting and gathering

Requirements

Fabric: Width 122 cm (48") – 70 cm ($27\frac{1}{2}$")
Lightweight polyester wadding: 43 cm (17") square
Mull muslin: 43 cm (17") square
Tacking cotton
Thread
Velcro: 30 cm (12")
Soft lead pencil
Cushion pad

Instructions

1 Draw/trace design or press transfer onto mull muslin.

2 Cut fabric as in diagram.

3 Place front piece of cushion cover, RS down, on flat surface, lay square of wadding next, then the mull muslin, having the design side up.

4 Pin along one edge and tack through all layers, starting in the centre and working outwards on both sides, smoothing the layers during tacking.

5 Having the mull muslin uppermost, machine the design using stitch length 4, with the quilting or embroidery foot in position.

6 Having RS up, machine again on previous stitching lines, using a satin stitch where appropriate.

7 Slightly round corners of front piece (see page 88).

8 Join ruffle lengths into a round, press seams open. Fold in two WS together, pin and tack.

9 Divide into four, mark with pins; work one row of gathering on the seam line 1.3 cm ($\frac{1}{2}''$), making a break of cotton at each pin.

10 Divide each section into two, mark with tacking.

11 With all threads through to the WS, pull up bobbin threads, making each gathering section an equal measurement of 40.5 cm (16").

12 Divide each side of cushion front into two, pin to mark. Place ruffle, having all raw edges together, with the break of gathering at the pins, and the tack marks on the ruffle at each corner. Adjust and even out the gathers; pin as shown, tack and machine.

13 Gather by hand, and tack down the folded edge of the ruffle at each corner – this will avoid it being caught in the stitching when machining the back in place.

14 Make back of cushion cover as in previous instructions for *Appliqué* cushions (steps 15–19, see page 89).

15 Place the front and back RS together; pin, tack and machine, using the stitch line for attaching the ruffle to the front as a guide.

16 Trim wadding and mull muslin to stitching line.

17 Snip into corners a little, turn to RS. Do not press.

Round

Round cushions compliment the square ones. Use a contrasting colour in the same fabric, choosing a shade to match the appliqué.

(**Note:** Machine Setting and Requirements from *Appliqué* and *Quilted* [see above] can be used.)

Instructions

1 Fold a square piece of paper in quarters. Make a pattern, following diagram, using pencil and string method for drawing a circle.

2 Cut fabric as in diagram.

3 Use piping or ruffle trim, following previous instructions for *Appliqué* or *Quilted*. Attach to the circle, having divided the circumference in four equal sections.

4 Make the back as for *Appliqué* cushion (steps 15–19).

5 Cut into a circle using the paper pattern.

6 Complete as before, snipping out Vs from seam allowance all round, before turning to RS.

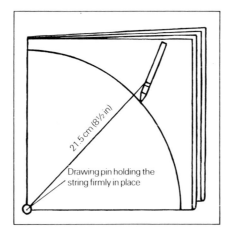

Round Cushion Cover *Drawing a circular pattern using pencil-and-string method.*

Plain, round cushion covers with piping and ruffle trim.

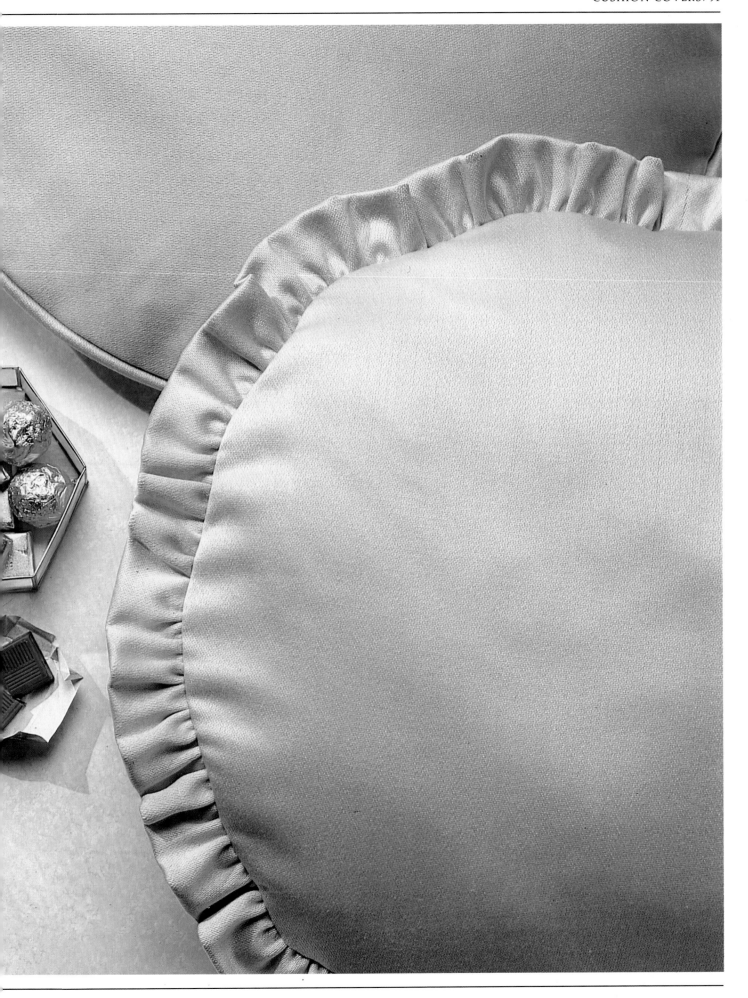

Round Cushion Cover *(Below) Cutting plan for cover and piping. (Bottom) Cutting plan for cover and ruffle.*

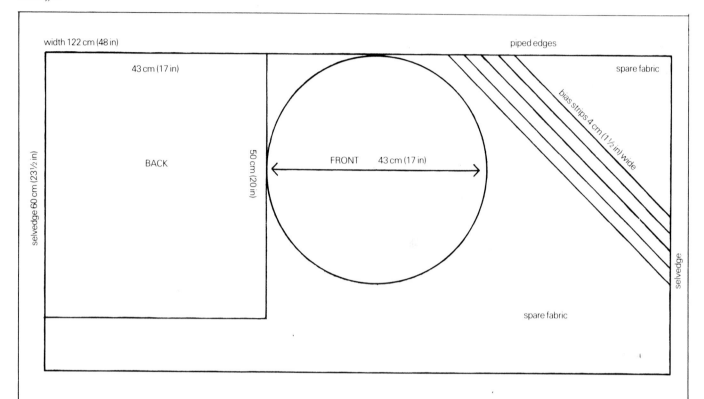

width 122 cm (48 in)

piped edges

43 cm (17 in)

spare fabric

selvedge 60 cm (23½ in)

BACK

50 cm (20 in)

FRONT   43 cm (17 in)

bias strips 4 cm (1½ in) wide

selvedge

spare fabric

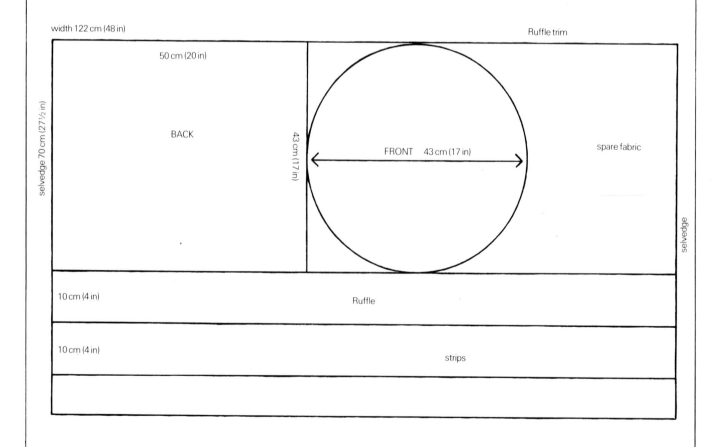

width 122 cm (48 in)

Ruffle trim

50 cm (20 in)

selvedge 70 cm (27½ in)

BACK

43 cm (17 in)

FRONT   43 cm (17 in)

spare fabric

selvedge

10 cm (4 in)   Ruffle

10 cm (4 in)   strips

4 Bedroom Accessories

Pretty cushions, matching hangers and pot-pourri sachets, give a feeling of luxury to a bedroom. All bedroom accessories make lovely gifts that will give pleasure both to the presenter and recipient alike.

Herb Pillow

Herb pillows serve a two-fold function depending on the content of their filling. The choice is quite vast, from the traditional hops to induce sleep, to the many pot-pourri mixtures which have a pleasant, sweeter aroma. The instructions for this herb pillow allows the cover to be removed for washing, and the pot-pourri, being in a separate muslin cover, can be replaced.

Pillow pad

1 Cut fabric for pillow pad, as in diagram.
2 Turn 1.3 cm ($\frac{1}{2}''$) on one edge of each piece; pin, tack and press.
3 With RS together, pin and machine the three other sides; trim corners and turn RS out.
4 Fill with polyester stuffing, using sufficient to make the pad quite plump. Machine stitch to close opening.

Machine setting

Presser foot: General/Zigzag
Needle: 80
Stitch width: 0 for straight stitch, and 2–2½ for zigzag
Stitch length: 2–2½ for stitching, and 4 for gathering

Requirements

Fabric–
Pillow cover: 70 cm ($27\frac{1}{2}''$) × 50 cm (20")
Pillow pad: Thin cotton 60 cm ($23\frac{1}{2}''$) × 35 cm (14")
Tacking cotton
Thread
Polyester stuffing
Butter muslin
Pot-pourri
Velcro: 20 cm (8")

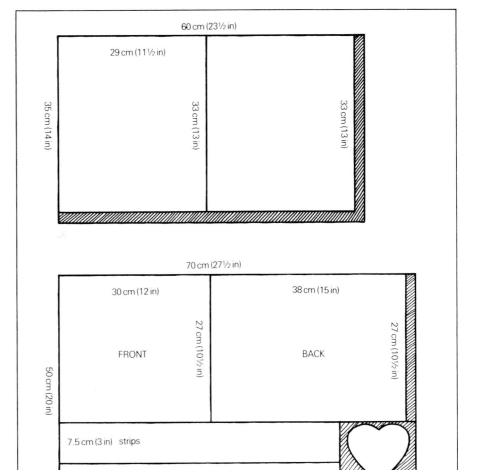

Herb Pillow *(Top) Cutting plan for pillow pad. (Above) Cutting plan for pillow cover and sachet.*

Note: Ruffle must be 1½ to 2 times the outside measurement of the pillow cover.

Pillow cover

1 Cut out pillow cover and ruffle (see diagram).
2 Place a pin to mark the centre of each side on front piece.
3 Join ruffle lengths into a round, using run and fell seam method.
4 Make a double turn, narrow hem along one edge.
5 Divide into four; mark with pins. Work one row of gathering 1.3 cm ($\frac{1}{2}''$) from raw edge, having a break of cotton at each pin.
6 Having all threads through to the WS, pull up bobbin threads, gathering each section up to 26 cm ($10\frac{1}{4}''$).

7 Position ruffle with the break of cotton at each pin on front piece, adjust and even out the gathers, ensuring there is sufficient fullness at the corners. Pin, tack and machine in place.
8 Gather by hand and tack down the folded edge of the ruffle at each corner – this will avoid it being caught in the machining when stitching the back in place.
9 Fold back of pillow cover in half and cut to make two pieces 19 cm ($7\frac{1}{2}''$) × 27 cm ($10\frac{1}{2}''$).
10 Neaten cut edges, and stitch Velcro in place (referring to page 89, steps 16–19, if necessary). Machine front and back together as in *Quilted Cushion* instructions.

Pot Pourri Sachet *Heart shape (actual size). Trace to make a pattern*

11 Cut a piece of muslin 40 cm (16″) × 20 cm (8″). Fold in half, to make a square, machine two sides. Turn RS out; fill with pot-pourri. Machine stitch to close.
12 Place pillow pad into the cover, and the pot-pourri sachet in the back before fastening.

Padded Hanger

Padded hangers can be made from any lightweight fabric. A set of hangers, matching other accessories in the bedroom, always looks attractive in the wardrobe. Alternatively, they can be made to match a garment, from the spare material left over, especially if it is a special occasion dress or blouse.

Padded Hanger *Cutting plan. Use a round object to make shape of curves.*

Instructions

1 Measure the hanger following the curve.
2 Cut a strip of material 15 cm (6″) longer than the hanger and 12.5 cm (5″) wide; also a bias strip 16.5 cm (6½″) × 2 cm (¾″).
3 Make a length of rouleau from the bias strip. Slip this onto the hook; neaten the end.
4 Cut wadding 3 cm (1¼″) longer than hanger measurement, and wide enough to overlap at the top.

5 Sit the hanger onto the middle of the wadding. Pull up, and sew the overlap from the hanger hook outwards on both sides – do not pull the thread tight.
6 Press under 1.3 cm (½″) on both long edges of the covering strip and fold in half lengthwise RS together. Curve the ends as shown in the diagram, machine and trim seam. Turn to RS. Fold in two to find the centre; mark with a pin.
7 Fit hanger into curved ends, ensuring the wadding stays in place. Position the centre pin by the hook.
8 Stitch the cover on the hanger by hand, starting in the centre working outwards on both sides using small stitches, and ruching the material up, as you progress. Fasten thread off securely.
9 Tie a ribbon bow at base of hook.

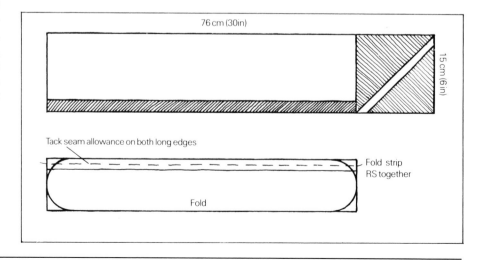

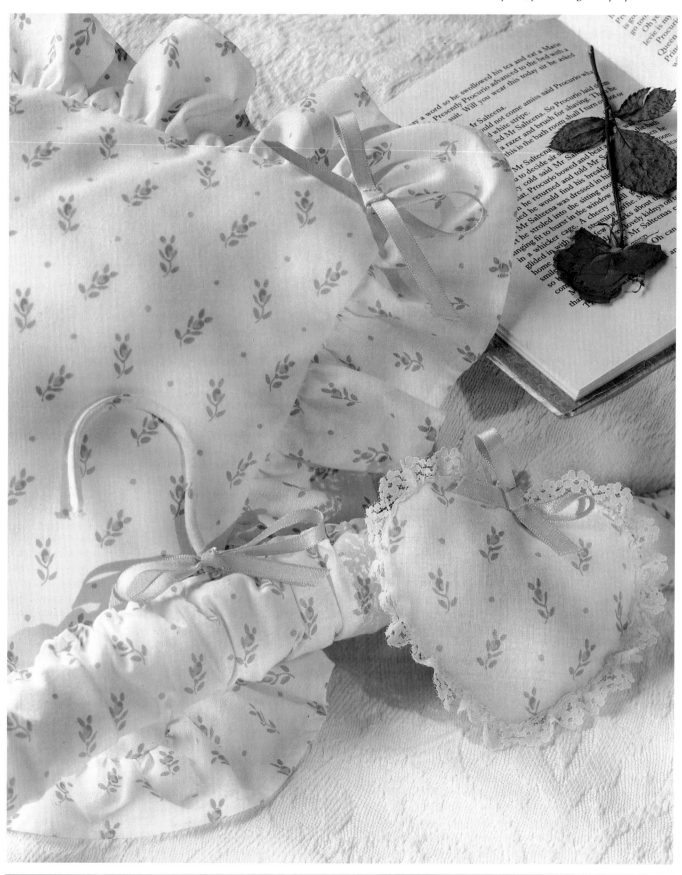

Herb pillow, padded hanger and pot-pourri sachet.

Bed Cushions

Placing cushions on a bed in the daytime gives an extra-caring look. They can appear expensive without necessarily being so. Ribbon and lace can be used in various ways to create a luxurious touch. Wide pink ribbon is used for the following cushion.

Machine setting

Presser foot: General/Zigzag
Needle: 80
Stitch width: 0 for straight stitch, and 2–2½ for zigzag
Stitch length: 2–2½ for stitching, and 4 for gathering

Requirements

Fabric: Width 115 cm (45″) – 50 cm (20″)
Interfacing: Ultrasoft light iron-on – 34.5 cm (13½″) square
Ribbon: 76 cm (3″) wide – 3.50 m (4 yds)
Lace: 5 cm (2″) wide – 2.30 m (2½ yds)
Velcro: 15 mm (⅝″) wide – 25 cm (10″)
Crystal beads
Tacking cotton
Thread
Cushion pad to fit

(**Note:** To facilitate pressing the ribbon onto the interfacing, choose a suitably padded board or table.)

Instructions

1 Place interfacing adhesive side down on a flat surface; mark position for first centre piece of ribbon (see diagram).
2 Pin interfacing, adhesive side up, on a padded board. Pin ribbon on interfacing, RS up, using the marked position, and cut to length.
3 Pin further ribbon lengths in the same direction on both sides of centre piece.
4 To form diagonal weave, start by positioning centre piece of ribbon from the opposite top corner, checking by measurement that it is in the centre. Weave under and over, lifting and lowering the ribbons as

you go. Pin in place at bottom corner.
5 Pin and weave ribbon lengths to complete the weaving – it will be necessary to pin and repin to do this.
6 Check that all the ribbon is correctly positioned; leave pins in place. Dry press using low heat setting on the iron, which will be sufficient to start sticking the ribbons to the interfacing.
7 Remove pins, carefully turn over the work. Press the back with a damp muslin and hotter iron. Leave to cool.
8 Cut out back and ruffle strips as in diagram.
9 Join ruffle strips into a round; press seams open. Fold in two lengthwise; tack raw edges together.
10 Join lace into a round, matching up the design if possible, having the same measurement length as the satin strip.
11 Tack lace over satin strip; divide into four sections, and mark with pins. Work one row of gathering 1.3 cm (½″) from raw edges, having a break of cotton at each pin.
12 Divide each section of the ruffle into two; mark with tacking.
13 With all threads through to the WS, pull up bobbin threads, to gather each section to an equal measurement of 32 cm (12½″).
14 Divide each side of cushion front into two; pin to mark. Place ruffle, having all raw edges together, with the break of gathering at the pins, then tack marks on the ruffle at each corner. Adjust and even out the gathers; pin as shown in diagram on page 88, tack and machine.
15 Gather by hand, and tack down the folded edge of the ruffle at each corner – this will avoid it being caught in the stitching when machining the back in place.
16 Fold back of cushion cover in half and cut to make two pieces 34.5 cm (13½″) × 21 cm (8¼″).
17 Neaten cut edges, and stitch Velcro in place (referring to page 89, steps 16–19, if necessary).
18 Stitch crystal beads at each corner of the squares, formed by the weaving of the ribbon.
19 Place front and back RS together; pin, tack and machine using the stitch line from attaching the ruffle to the front as a guide. Take out tacking.
20 Snip into corners a little; turn to RS. Then remove tacking from ruffle at each corner.

P78

Ribbon and Lace Trimmed Cushion

Made to the same dimensions as the previous cushion cover, the trimming is a collection of ribbon, satin and taffeta, and lace of varying widths, machined onto a piece of polyester/cotton, with iron-on interfacing on the back. The trim is stitched on the diagonal using zigzag. The lace and ribbon ruffle is purchased and sewn on the outside edge after the cushion cover is completed.

Pot-pourri Sachets

Sachets can be made any shape for filling with sweet smelling pot-pourri. Lace or ribbon trimming gives an extra feminine touch. To make a matching set consisting of a cushion, padded hanger and sachet for a present is more than pleasing.

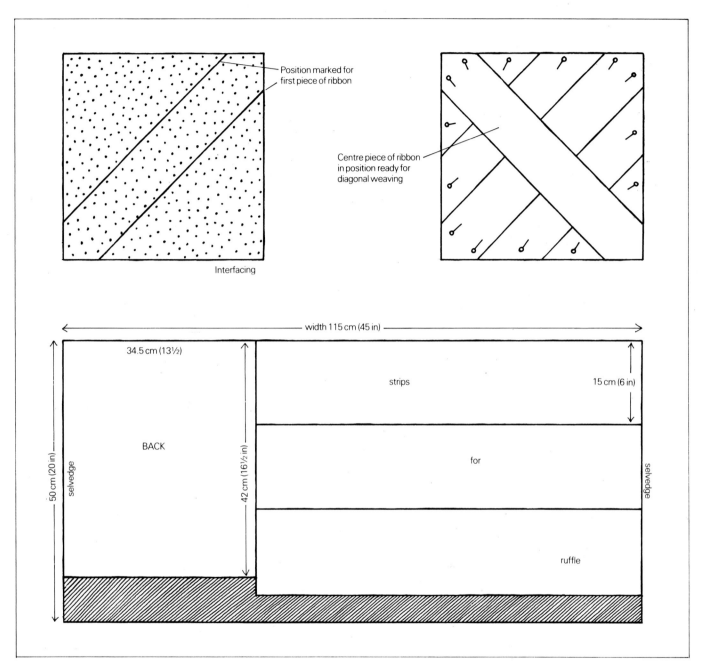

Ribbon-weaving Cushion Cover *(Top)*
Ribbon-weaving diagrams. (Above) Cutting plan
for cushion back and ruffle.

5 Baby Specials

It is always delightful to make baby items, whether they are for use in your own family, or to give as gifts. Searching for pretty pastel fabrics and musing over trims is satisfying to most, and the thought of turning the fabric into useful things even more so.

Quilt and Pillowcase

Designed for a pram or carrycot, the quilt can easily be adapted to other sizes by drawing a diagram on squared paper of the dimensions required, and calculating fabric to be purchased by making a cutting-out plan. The pillowcases, broderie anglaise trimmed, is very simply made from measurements.

Machine setting

Presser feet: General/Zigzag and Quilting
Needle: 80–90
Stitch width: 0
Stitch length: 2–4

Requirements

Fabric: Width 115 cm (45″) – 1.50 m (1⅝ yds) main design, and 30 cm (12″) each of four contrasting colours
Ultrasoft light iron-on
Thick polyester wadding: 64 cm (25″) × 53 cm (21″)
Broderie Anglaise: 2 m (2¼ yds) (raw edges)
Tacking cotton
Thread
Elastic
Safety pillow pad: 35 cm (14″) × 30 cm (12″)

(**Note:** 1.3 cm (½″) seam allowance is included in the measurements given for cutting out the back of the quilt, and the pillowcase. There will be fabric left over from this set, which can be used for lining the Toilet Basket.)

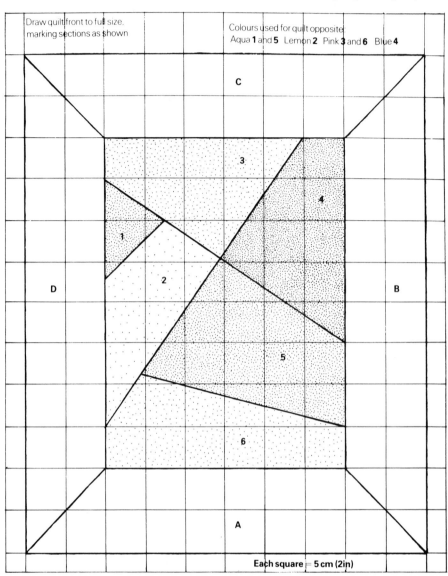

Baby's Quilt *Diagram pattern.*

Draw quilt front to full size, marking sections as shown

Colours used for quilt opposite:
Aqua **1** and **5** Lemon **2** Pink **3** and **6** Blue **4**

C

3

4

1

2

B

D

5

6

A

Each square = 5 cm (2in)

Quilt

1 Draw the quilt front to full size on squared pattern paper. Mark the sections with numbers or letters as shown, and cut on drawn lines.
2 Press interfacing to pieces of contrasting fabric large enough to cut out the sections with 6 mm (¼″) turnings, taking care that the straight grain of fabric will be on the length of the quilt.
3 Cut out shapes marking the cutting line on the fabric, allowing 6 mm (¼″) turnings.
4 Cut out pieces required in the main fabric, following the measurements on the cutting-out diagram, for quilt back and pillowcase. Using the border pattern pieces, mark the cutting line on the fabric allowing 6 mm (¼″)

on inside seams and 1.3 cm (½″) on the outer edges.
5 Pin, tack and machine the coloured sections in the following order, pressing each seam before proceeding to the next:

1 to 2;   1 and 2 to 3;
4 to 5;   4 and 5 to 6;
1,2 and 3 to 4, 5, and 6.

6 Press interfacing to border pieces, and with RS together machine the diagonal seams, sewing from the outward to inner corners, finishing 6 mm (¼″) from the corners, and in the following sequence: A to B; B to C; C to D; then D to A. Press seams open.

Baby's quilt and pillowcase.

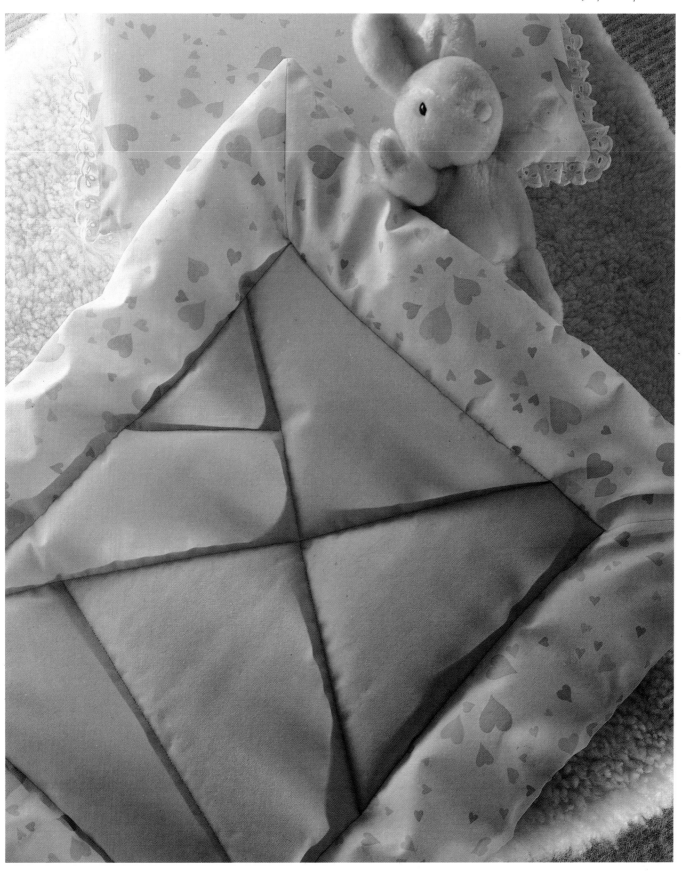

Baby's Quilt and Pillowcase *Cutting plan for main fabric with RS uppermost.*

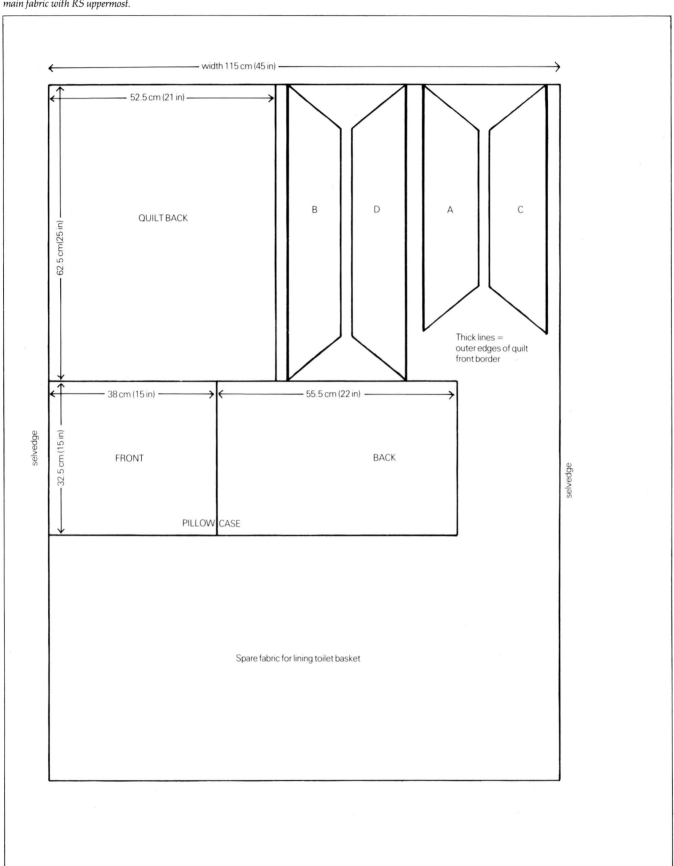

Baby's Quilt *Machining border to centre panel.*

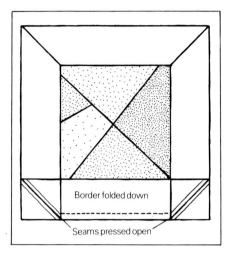

Border folded down

Seams pressed open

Toilet Basket 1 *First method (round basket) – measure the inside of the basket as shown. Take half this measurement, plus seam allowance, to make a circular pattern using the pencil-and-string method* (see p.90). **2** *Second method (any shape basket) – to make a pattern for the bottom of the lining, draw around the base of the basket.*

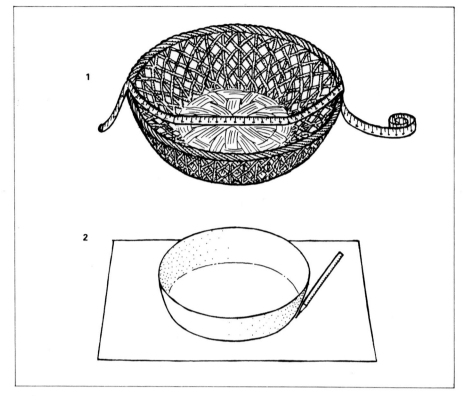

7 With RS together stitch the border to the centre panel, working with the border on top and folding it to allow the machining to be worked on each side separately in the direction of the following order: A to 6; B to 6, 5 and 4; D to 6, 2, 1 and 3; C to 3 and 4. Press seams open.
8 Tack wadding to WS of quilt front, keeping fabric smooth – it will be necessary to tack both length and width.
9 Place back to front, RS together; pin, tack and machine 1.3 cm (½″) from raw edges, leaving a 25 cm (10″) gap on one side. Trim wadding back to the stitching, and the seams to 6 mm (¼″).
10 Turn quilt RS out and slip stitch gap securely. Without using any pressure, smooth with warm iron, if necessary.
11 Tack through all layers before machine quilting the centre panel, by 'stitching in the ditch' (page 17).
12 Take out all tacking.

Pillowcase

1 Apply broderie anglaise to the front piece of the pillowcase using the same method as the ruffle on the quilted cushion cover (page 88).
2 Turn a double narrow hem using 1.3 cm (½″) along the 32.5 cm (13″) edge of both the back pieces.
3 With RS up, overlap the neatened edges 7.5 cm (3″) and tack.
4 Position back to the front, RS together. Pin, tack, machine, trim seams and corners. Take out tacking of overlap, turn to RS, press seam edge.

Toilet Basket

Baskets come in all sorts of shapes and sizes, so only the principle of lining them can be given. A very simple method, using a double layer of fabric with ribbon ties, is quick to make, yet looks attractive. For a more elaborate touch, work quilting on the lining pieces, lace trim the pockets and add a ruffle to hang over the sides of the basket.

A round basket, with sloping sides, and an open weave top, is ideal for the first method.

1 To find the diameter measurement for the two circles required, measure the inside of the basket in the centre, by laying the tape measure from the top down the side, along the bottom and up the opposite side to the top.
2 Make a pattern for the circles, using pencil and string method (page 90), adding 1.3 cm (½″) seam allowance.
3 Cut out in fabric; stitch 6 ribbon ties at equal distances round the circumference of one circle, (use more ties if it is a large basket).
4 Place circles RS together, tack and machine round, leaving a 10 cm (4″) opening.

Snip Vs out from seam allowance.
5 Turn through and hand stitch gap closed. Roll seam to edge and edge stitch, press.
6 Place in basket and tie ribbons to the top.

Items placed in the basket will keep the lining in position, although if the basket weave is loose enough to allow a needle to pass through, the base can be stitched down.

When using the second method any shape basket can be used.
1 Stand the basket on paper to make a pattern. Draw round the base, add 1.3 cm (½″) seam allowance.
2 For the sides measure the top circumference, add seam allowance. Measure depth of basket, on the inside, and add 6 cm (2½″), which includes seam allowance on both edges.
3 Cut out the bottom and sides in fabric, wadding and lining.
4 Machine the fabric for the sides into a round, also the lining. Place the RS together, machine along one edge. Turn RS out, tack and press.
5 Prepare for quilting. The bottom requires the three layers to be tacked together in the normal way. For the sides, place the wad-

ding, 1.3 cm ($\frac{1}{2}$"), below the stitched top edge between the fabric and lining, tack.

6 Stay-stitch, using stitch length 4, just within the seam allowance of the bottom edge. Trim away surplus wadding to the stitch line.

7 Work freehand quilting on the bottom and sides, avoiding going nearer than 3 cm ($1\frac{1}{4}$") from the top of the sides.

8 Edge stitch top and work another row of machining 1 cm ($\frac{3}{8}$") below, to form a hem for elastic to be inserted later.

9 Using half the circumference measurement, cut twice in contrasting fabric for the pockets, calculating the finished depth, including a lace trim, 1 cm ($\frac{3}{8}$") less than the actual basket depth – remember a seam allowance will be required top and bottom of the pockets.

10 Insert lace to sides and top pocket strip; turn RS out, press and edge stitch.

11 Place to the RS of the side lining, raw edges together, tack in place. Machine to form pockets (see diagram).

12 Divide sides into two and work gathering thread. Mark with tacking halfway between each section.

13 Divide base into four and mark.

14 Having all threads through to the WS, pull up bobbin threads to gather side to fit the base, matching the section marks. Position the pockets as you wish (it depends on the shape of the basket), tack and machine. Trim seam to 6 mm ($\frac{1}{4}$"), zigzag to neaten.

15 Placing basket on a table, measure on the outside, from the top to the table to determine the depth of the ruffle, which will be stitched to the side lining to coincide with the top of the basket. Add 4 cm ($1\frac{1}{2}$") to this measurement.

16 Cut ruffle $1\frac{1}{2}$ times circumference measurement by the calculated depth.

17 Machine ruffle into a round. Make a narrow double hem, using 1 cm ($\frac{3}{8}$") for the bottom edge; tack and machine.

18 Make a double hem using 3 cm ($1\frac{1}{4}$") on the other edge for the top. Tack.

19 Divide ruffle into four and work gathering threads along the edge of the tacked hem.

20 Divide the quilted side into four and mark with tacking. Sit the lining into the basket and determine the top by measuring; tack round at this measurement which will be the seam line for stitching the ruffle into position.

21 Gathering ruffle to fit, place on marked line, tack and machine.

22 Insert elastic into hem of sides, and stitch four ribbon ties to base seam on the WS.

23 Thread the ribbons through the basket weave at the bottom and tie. Slip the elasticated hem over the top.

24 Make a heart-shaped pin cushion, trimming with lace to match the pockets; stuff very firmly with polyester filling. Stitch a bow on the front and a length of ribbon at the back for attaching to the side of the lining.

25 A cover could be made to match the lining.

Baby's toilet basket. For pin-cushion use heart-shaped pattern, page 94.

Rainbow Wall Hanging *(opposite) Lightly draw the picture on to the prepared fabric. Dotted line indicates hem allowance.*

6 Miscellaneous

All the items under this last heading have been designed for a 'special' use. The bright and cheerful Rainbow Wall Hanging will appeal to children and teach them to appreciate colour. The Sewing and Knitting Bag will keep craft work, clean, neat and tidy. The Sewing Machine Cover will keep your machine dust free, but will allow instant use.

Rainbow Wall Hanging

Instructions

Note: Prepare a testing piece with spare fabric in the same way as for project. Thread matching the fabric is used on the bobbin throughout.

1 Cut one piece of fabric, and one piece of interfacing 50 cm (20") × 38 cm (15").

Machine setting

Presser feet: General and Embroidery
Needle: 90
Stitch width: 0 for straight stitch, $2\frac{1}{2}$–$3\frac{1}{2}$ for rainbow, and 2–4 for decorative stitches
Stitch length: 2–$2\frac{1}{2}$ for straight stitch, and nearly 0–$\frac{1}{2}$ for embroidery

Requirements

Fabric: Calico or similar, sufficient to cut piece required
Interfacing: Ultrasoft medium iron-on
Stitch'n'Tear
Thread: Matching fabric, varigated and colours
Tacking cotton
Dowelling and knobs
Cord for hanging

2 Press interfacing to WS of the fabric, and tack Stitch'n'Tear to the back.

3 Lightly draw the design onto RS of top fabric using a soft lead pencil or fabric pen, with sufficient detail to guide working the picture – the lines will be covered with the embroidery.

4 Try out selected stitches on your test piece, adjusting length and width of stitch setting as necessary. The top tension will probably require loosening a little.

5 Work the pathway, tree, fields, cloud and sun, cloud and rain with the appropriate colour and pre-set decorative stitches. Work rainbow in satin stitch, using the colours of the spectrum: red, orange, yel-

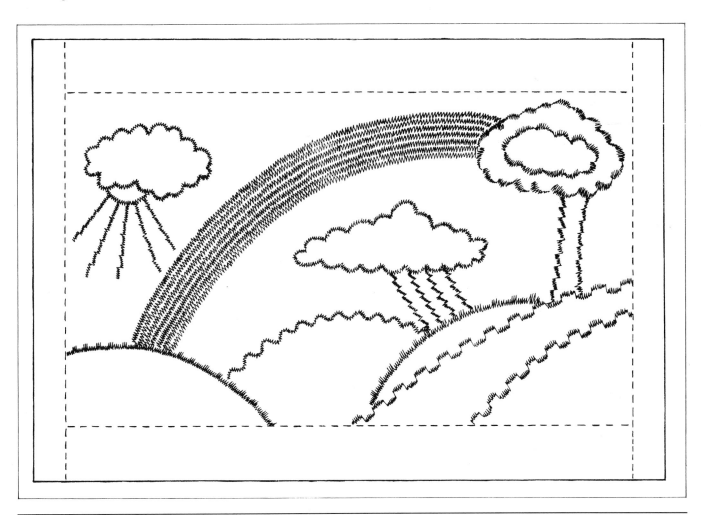

low, green, blue, indigo and violet.

6 Place work RS down on a thick pad, press with a damp muslin. Leave to cool and dry.

7 Turn side hems 2.5 cm (1″) single turn, edge stitch, trim and press.

8 Turn top and bottom hems 4 cm (1½″) single turn, machine and press.

9 Insert dowelling through casings, attach knobs. Knot cord into place ready for hanging.

Quilted Sewing or Knitting Bag

Instructions

1 Cut out bag, self lining and handle bands.

2 Cut two pieces of wadding 48 cm (19″) × 50 cm (20″).

3 Prepare the three layers for quilting (self-lining, wadding and fabric) for front and back.

4 Quilt in freehand style, following or going round the design on the fabric.

5 Machine all edges using zigzag.

6 Neaten the side edges, on front and back,

Machine setting

Presser feet: General/Zigzag and Quilting
Needle: 90
Stitch width: 0 straight stitch, and 3–4 zigzag
Stitch length: 2½–3 seaming, and 3–4 zigzag and quilting

Requirements

Fabric: Border Print width 115 cm (45″) – 1 m (1⅛ yds)
Interfacing: Ultrasoft Light iron-on – 30 cm (12″) × 20 cm (8″)
Lightweight polyester wadding: 100 cm (39″) wide – 50 cm (20″)
Tacking cotton
Thread: Matching and contrasting
Bias binding: 2.5 cm (1″) wide – 2 m (2¼ yds)
Wooden handles with slots
Cardboard for base
Fabric glue

Quilted Sewing or Knitting Bag 1 *Cutting plan using a border print fabric.* **2** *Bottom seam of bag.* **3** *On bottom seam stitch from fold to fold 5 cm (2 in) from the point to give a base of 10 cm (4 in).*

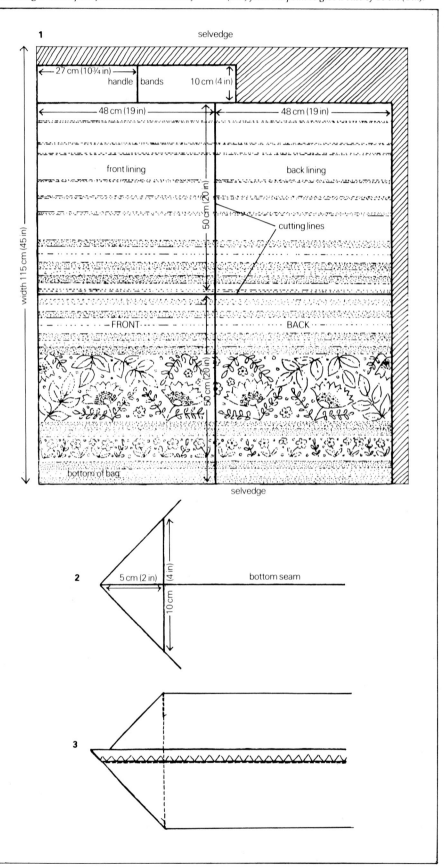

for 14 cm (5½″) from the top, with bias binding.

7 Machine seams, starting 12 cm (4¾″) from top on one side, along the bottom and finishing 12 cm (4¾″) from the top on the other side.

8 Neaten seams with bias binding.

9 Turn to WS. Fold bottom of bag as in diagram. Stitch from fold to fold, on both sides, to form the base.

10 Gather by hand, using double sewing thread, along the top of front and back.

11 Press interfacing to WS of bands.

12 Turn ends of bands in 1 cm (⅜″), machine and press. Place them, RS to outside of gathered front and back, adjust gathers. Tack and machine. Press seam towards band.

13 Turn 1 cm (⅜″) on raw edge of band, tack and press.

14 Thread the prepared edges of bands through the slots of the handles. Hem in place neatening the seam.

15 Cut a piece of thick cardboard to the size of the base, and cover with material, glueing it into place.

Sewing Machine Cover

Instructions

1 Measure your sewing machine at the widest point, for width, height and depth.

2 Make a diagram plan using your measurements, adding for the ease 2.5 cm (1″) to the width and height, 1.3 cm (½″) to the depth, plus 6 mm (¼″) on the seams.

3 Cut out twice in fabric and once in wadding, either by marking the cutting lines with tailor's chalk on your material, or by making a paper pattern.

4 Draw or trace the outline of the sewing machine onto the RS of one piece of fabric.

5 Prepare the three layers (fabric, wadding, fabric), for each section of the cover, for quilting.

6 Machine quilt the drawn outline of the sewing machine, with contrasting thread. Quilt any other area of the cover you wish, with either freehand or symmetrical design using matching thread.

Machine setting

Presser feet: General/Zigzag and Quilting
Needle: 90
Stitch width: 0 straight stitch, and 3–4 for zigzag
Stitch length: 3–4 for straight stitch, and 2½–3½ for zigzag

Requirements

Fabric and Wadding: calculate from measurements
Bias binding: 2.5 cm (1″) wide, in contrasting colour to fabric
Tacking cotton
Thread: Matching fabric and binding

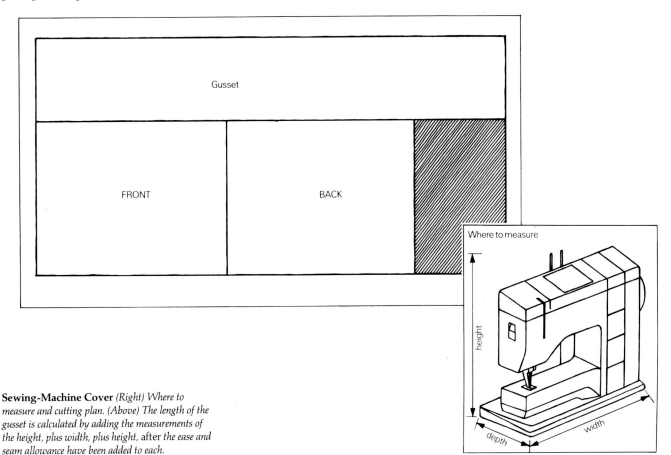

Sewing-Machine Cover *(Right) Where to measure and cutting plan. (Above) The length of the gusset is calculated by adding the measurements of the height, plus width, plus height, after the ease and seam allowance have been added to each.*

Sewing machine cover.

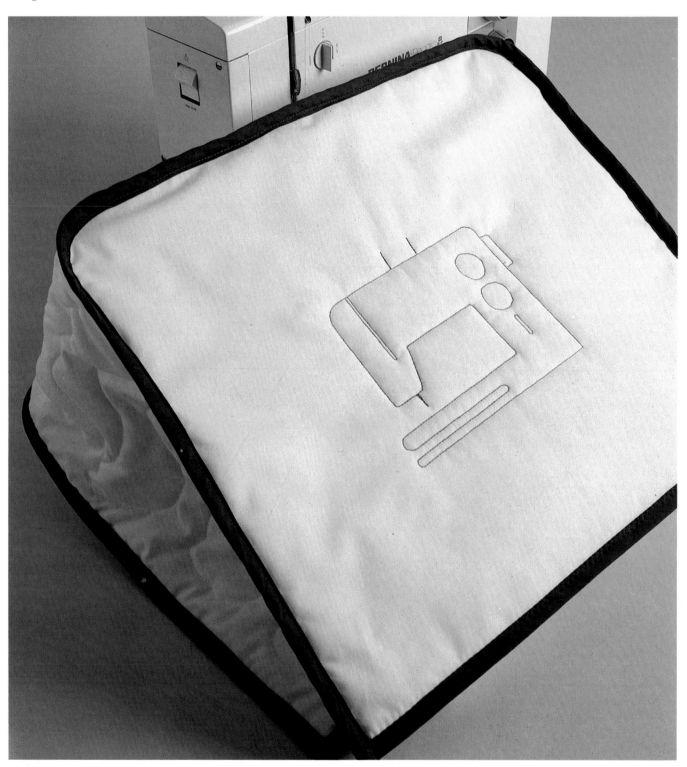

7 Round the top corners of front and back pieces.

8 Machine all edges using zigzag.

9 Because the top corners have been rounded, check the length of the gusset, on the seam line with either front or back to make sure it isn't too long; adjust if necessary.

10 Fold bias binding in two and press.

11 Apply to the bottom of front, back and narrow edges of gusset. Slot the edge into the fold of the bias. Tack, machine and zigzag.

12 Pin, tack; machine the gusset in place, having the seams on the outside.

13 Press bias binding to the shape of the corners and apply to the seams, neatening the ends by turning in 6 mm ($\frac{1}{4}$").

Index